Kuklinski

Kuklinski
The Devil Himself

J Sutton

The sources used to verify events were a combination of police, court and FBI records, newspaper articles, testimonies from his family and police officers dealing with his case, direct testimony from Richard himself totalling, 17 hours of interviews that were recorded for episodes of an HBO series; and a biographical based book written by Anthony Bruno.

Sources retrieved for the purpose of research where the person has now passed on have been verified to the best of my ability.

News articles sourced from archives where the journalist has passed on are taken in good faith to be accurate and account for actual events. Where possible they have been corroborated with police/court documentation.

Claims made by Richard Kuklinski during interviews, unless verified by evidence, cannot be accounted for as fact but as opinion only.

www.criminalbehaviours.com

Contents

Bonus Content

Reference Section

Introduction

New Jersey is said to have a devil that lurks in the Pine Barron of the South. This creature has been in tales of superstition for many years, creating both fear and curiosity. A myth fuelled by alleged sightings and rumours passed on from generation to generation.

This isn't the only case of a devil in New Jersey surrounded by rumour and suggestion, if you ventured north towards Dumont you would come to the home of another New Jersey Devil, a very real devil, one feared by many and confronted by none.

A 6ft 4, 240lb man with many names. Known to some as The Devil Himself to others he is the Iceman, the mafia called him The Pollack, and his friends knew him as Big Rich, to his wife he was Richie and Dad to his children. But the rest of the world would know him as Richard Kuklinski, mafia hitman and ruthless killer.

This is his story, his family's story and the story of his victims. The tragic events that led Richard to become the man he is known as today and the aftermath of his crimes.

Richard Leonard Kuklinski, is more famously known as The Iceman, he was a convicted killer. He had a history of violence and aggressive behaviours that occurred throughout his life. Over the years Richard has attracted great public interest, with many documentaries being filmed about him. He has taken part in interviews and even had a film made about his life.

Richards life began In New Jersey and ended there. He left a trail of pain and destruction wherever he went.

Richard began life as a victim of violence and abuse at the hands of his parents and went on to become a perpetrator of the same thing as an adult.

The actual number of murders he committed is not known and there is much speculation over some of the murders he has claimed to his name. He was convicted of 5 murders in total, however suspected to have committed many more.

Overall, Richard was a career criminal and was involved in varying types of organised crime. His criminal activity ranged from murder, theft, bootlegging, extortion, assault, domestic violence, and fraud.

The time frame of his criminal career spans roughly 37 years from 1949 - 1986. His first crime was theft around the age of 13 or14, he was never caught or convicted for this. His last known crime was conspiracy/attempted murder. It was this that led to the arrest of Kuklinski in 1986 and was achieved via an undercover operation led by the FBI.

The sources used to verify events were a combination of police; court and FBI records, newspaper articles, testimonies from his family and police officers dealing with his case, direct testimony from Richard himself totalling to 17 hours of interviews that were recorded for episodes of an HBO series and a biographical based book written by Anthony Bruno.

Sources retrieved for the purpose of research where the person has now passed on have been verified to the best of my ability. News articles sourced from archives where the journalist has passed on are taken in good faith to be accurate and account for actual events. Where possible they have been corroborated with police/court documentation.

Claims made by Richard Kuklinski during interviews, unless verified by evidence cannot be accounted for as fact but as opinion only.

Sources and references with public access can be found at the end of the book with links. Some sources cannot be published with links due to them being unavailable to the public. They can be retrieved upon request (some for a fee) from the state or library archives cited at the end.

Short Bio

Name	Richard Leonard Kuklinski
Date of Birth	11th April 1935 - Jersey City, New Jersey USA
Place of Birth	222 Third Street in Jersey City, New Jersey
Date of Death	March 5, 2006 (aged 70) Died of natural causes (Death deemed suspicious by some)
Physical Disposition	roughly 300lbs, 6'4ft
Ancestry	Polish and Irish descent
Father	Stanisław (Stanley) Kuklinski (1906 - 1977) a Polish immigrant from Karwacz, Masovian Voivodeship (East central Poland) worked as railroad break-man in New Jersey.
Mother	Maiden name - Anna McNally Marital Name Anna Kuklinski (1911–1972) Irish descent from Harsimus in New Jersey. Worked as a meat packer. Strict catholic.
Siblings	Brother Florian (1933–1941) Died from a beating by the hand of Stanley Kuklinski death officially recorded as bronchopneumonia, Sister Roberta Florence Kuklinski (1942–2010), Brother Joseph Michael Kuklinski (1944–2003)
Spouses	2 -1st Wife Linda Kuklinski (divorced) - 2nd Wife Barbara Kuklinksi (estranged/ex)

Children	5 - 2 boys from his 1st marriage, 2 girls and 1 boy from his 2nd marriage.
Tactics	Con man, Thief, Bootlegger, Contract killer, Debt collector
Victim Pool	Males age 18+
Victim Type	Business partners/potential business partners of Kuklinski, 1 homicide was a police officer, he claimed this was a hit for the Gambino crime family.
Murder Count	He has claimed multiple murders (200+) however many of his claims cannot be substantiated or there is not enough evidence to link him to the crime for a conviction to be possible. Convicted of 5 counts of murder.
Modus Operandi	Richard had two distinct motives for killing these can be accounted for separately and are situational - Monetary and control/power/paranoia. Mixture of disorganised and organised crimes
Address at time of arrest	169 Sunset St, Dumont, NJ 07628. USA
Date of Arrest	17th December 1986
Charges	5 counts of murder, 6 weapons violations, Attempted murder, Robbery, Attempted robbery
Convicted	25 March 1988

Timeline

- 1935 – 11th April Richard Leonard Kuklinski is born
- 1942 – Richards sister Roberta Kuklinski is born
- 1942 – Richards father leaves the home he would return periodically.
- 1944 – Richards brother Joseph Kuklinski is born
- 1949 – Richards alleged 1st murder age 14
- 1950 – Richard drops out of high school
- 1953 – Richard becomes associated to members of the Mafia
- 1958 – Richard is arrested with stolen goods Jersey City NJ
- 1960 – Richard gets a job at the Swiftline Trucking company
- 1960 – Richard and Barbara meet and start dating
- 1961 – 8th September Barbara and Richard get married
- 1964 – 27th March 1st daughter is born
- 1965 – 21st April 2nd daughter is born
- 1965/1981 – Got involved with Roy DeMeo – borrowed money – alleged to have worked as a contract killer for the Gambino crime family.
- 1969 – 13th January 3rd child is born a son.
- 1969 – Joseph Kuklinski arrested and charged for rape and murder of a minor.
- 1971 – December 24th Bruno Latini murdered NYC
- 1980 – February 1st Geoge Malliband murdered NJ
- 1980 – March 14th Peter Calabro murdered NJ
- 1981 – July 1st Louis Masgay murdered NJ
- 1981 – Lieutenant Pat Kane begins investigation into burglary gang

- 1982 – April 29th Paul Hoffman murdered NJ
- 1982 – December Gary Smith murdered NJ
- 1983 – February Daniel Deppner murdered NJ
- 1984 – August Robert Prongay murdered NJ
- 1985 – Operation Iceman begins
- 1986 – Richard is arrested 17th December
- 1988 – March Richards Trial commences
- 1988 – March 25th Richard is convicted of Gary and Daniels murders
- 1991 – filmed interviews for HBO
- 2001 – Richard confessed to the murder of Peter Calabro
- 2003 – convicted of Peter Calabros murder.
- 2006 – March 5th Richard Died, recorded as a natural death.

1

Childhood
and
family life
1935 – 1949

"My mother was cancer. She slowly destroyed
everything around her.
She produced two killers; me and my brother
Joe."
Richard Kuklinski

Richard grew up in the New Jersey projects in Jersey City, at the time this housing was allocated for immigrants. The population around the project housing was largely Italian, Irish, and Polish.

This was a poverty-stricken area, so addiction, domestic violence, and crime was rife. For immigrants at the time there was not many work opportunities, so a lot of people resorted to crime in order to survive. And would use alcohol to drown their sorrows.

Richards father Stanley was a Polish immigrant who had come to the USA in search of the American dream. But on arrival found that those from places like Poland, Ireland, Sicily, and Italy were not considered as equals. They were shunned by American society, used for cheap labour, and treated like outsiders. As a result of this there was not many ways a family like Richards could make good money or afford good housing.

His father was abusive verbally and physically to both the mother and children. He would regularly beat Richard, this began at a young age. He was also a drunk, causing the beatings to occur more often when under the influence.

Richard recalls his father disrespecting his mother by bringing home other women at times. During one of these occasions Richard had yelled at his father and told him to stop. This resulted in Richard receiving a bad beating from Stanley, worse than normal. After this had happened and Richards mother had not tried to stop his father from doing this, he no longer tried to prevent things like that from happening.

Stanley abandoned the family shortly after Richards sister Roberta was born, when Richard was around the age of 7 or 8. This affected Richard, he disliked his father due to the abuse, but this made him hate and resent him.

Richards mother Anna was of Irish descent, she had been raised as an orphan in a children's home. Coming from a strict catholic environment where discipline and routine was prioritised over love and affection. This meant Anna never really learned how to be a loving parent.

Growing up without much affection herself Anna found it hard to be the maternal mother her children craved. She was stubborn, cold, and unaffectionate. Often, she would also resort to verbal abuse and violence when disciplining her own children.

He came from a strict catholic household which was mainly pushed via his mother. He attended a catholic grammar school and was an altar boy.

Richard stated that after his father abandoned the family, he would periodically show up at the family home (for short periods of time). During these times he would drink, verbally abuse, and beat the children. This mostly occurred while his mother was at work, however Richard recalls times his mother was present. He said at times she would yell at his father to try to get him to stop hitting the children, but this would only cause his father to stop momentarily.

His father would eventually leave again after the birth of his brother Joseph and not be seen for prolonged periods of time. He describes visiting his father's workplace as a young boy in the hopes to catch a glimpse of him at times.

His mother Anna was also verbally, emotionally, and physically abusive. She was also negligent in the children's general care and due to financial issues was unable to provide the children with proper clothing or food.

His mother worked as a meat packer in a warehouse, therefore was not at home much in the day times. In the evenings she would go to the church to help clean there and do odd jobs for them. The amount of time she spent at home with her children was little.

During the times she was at home she rarely interacted with the children, other than to discipline them. She would often fall asleep listening to the radio, leaving Richard and his siblings to their own devices, causing there to be no real structure or routine in his home life.

Her discipline at times was just as harsh as his fathers. Richard recounts occasions where she used a broom stick to hit him with, he states that one time it even broke when she hit it off his body.

The verbal and emotional abuse carried out by Anna in Richards opinion was worse than the physical punishments given to him by his father. According to Richard, these verbal assaults had a profound effect on his self-esteem and self-worth.

He expresses a great distaste for his mother. He said she would give the children little to no attention or affection and was a very hard-faced woman.

During times where families would normally celebrate such as Christmases and birthdays, Richard would often see he was missing out. He saw how other children his age would get parties or gifts; their families would decorate their homes at Christmas and all gather together. He longed for this, he longed to be just like them, even if it was only for a passing moment.

It was coming up to the day of Richards communion, he thought that maybe his mother, a devout Catholic woman would see this as a special day. She might make an effort Richard thought to himself. But for Richard the day came and went like any other.

His mother didn't even show up to his communion. He watched on as the other children's families gathered around them to congratulate them, many of them in new clothes, sporting new watches. He was feeling left out, let down and forgotten, he knew if his mother hadn't cared about this, she really didn't care at all.

Socially, Richard did not make friends easily and does not seem to recount any lasting friendships growing up. He does, however, describe being bullied by his peers, one boy specifically stands out for him (un-named).

In his local neighbourhood he describes a boy who would regularly bully him, this boy would publicly humiliate Richard on a regular basis. Richard describes being scared to go out in case he bumped into this boy. He said the way he was treated by him had a lasting effect, it led to him feeling very insecure about things such as his appearance and his family's overall wealth. He describes hating this boy with a passion.

His nurture-less environment meant Richard did not fully develop skills such as compassion or empathy. Little physical affection meant his tactile development also suffered. Any form of rejection from a parent, especially early on in a child's life, is known to have detrimental negative effects on mental development and mental health later in life.

Richard's criminal and deviant behaviour began to occur around the age of 9 or 10 years old, he would truant from school and start to hang about the local area. It seems his father leaving was a trigger and contribution to this.

This type of behaviour is not unusual for children experiencing abandonment issues. The symptoms for this can result in feelings of rejection, low self-esteem, anxiety, anger, lack of emotional intimacy and intensify the need to be accepted by others.

They will often seek acceptance from those outside of the family unit, such as peers. Often, due to the child's vulnerability, their behaviours can become more extreme as time goes on. They will seek to be accepted by less desirable members of society such as gangs. Gangs who will take advantage of the person and manipulate them into a life of crime.

2

Early Teens

1949 – 1955

Richard recalls committing his first crime as a young teen around the age of 13 – 14. This was the theft of a crate of wine. After stealing the wine he had hidden it, unsure what to do with it. He expresses feeling paranoid that he would be caught and felt as though everybody knew what he had done.

This intense paranoia led to feelings of sickness, loss of appetite and restlessness. This continued for a while until a few weeks had passed and he started to come to the realisation that he had gotten away with it. Once he had got over his initial bout of paranoia, he started to feel more confident about what he had done.

This would be the start of a long criminal career of theft, after this initial crime Richard had gained confidence in his ability to steal. He would begin to steal things which he could then sell on. This meant he had a bit of money to buy the things his mother and father wouldn't or couldn't afford.

This wasn't the only anti-social behaviour Richard would display, around the same age he started inflicting harm on animals. Mostly cats and dogs around the local area.
From time to time if he came across an animal, he would torture them and often kill them. It is important to state that he would not always watch the animals suffering or their death.

In some cases, he would merely put the animal in a position of suffering then leave them to struggle or die. It was the idea that he had control of their fate, he said he didn't feel pleasure from the act itself but enjoyed the feeling of complete control. He claimed that was the motivation for these actions, coupled with curiosity.

Ultimately, he sought out to have power over them and this gave him a sense of satisfaction.

For example, in the interviews for HBO, Richard talks about tying dogs to the back of bus carts by a leash so the dog would have to run behind the bus cart. Eventually, the dog would get too tired and was dragged along until it died. When asked if he watched this, he stated, that he would just tie the dogs and leave, not looking to see the end result of his actions. He claimed he did these things out of boredom.

There was an incident where he tied two cats together by their tails and hung them from a clothesline. Leaving them to fight each other. He said he watched them fight for a while, got bored, and then left.

There were times he did discuss watching the animal suffer to the death, for example in the case of cats, he would throw them into incinerators and watch how they reacted to the flames. He would also kick dogs off roofs to watch them hit the floor and die. He explained it gave him momentary excitement, but it would eventually lead to a feeling of disgust.

These violent tendencies weren't something he did to just animals, as Rich got older he started to tower over his peers. He began to realise that he could stick up for himself, he didn't have to take the taunts of bullies or the hits dished out by them. That he could be the one giving the taunts and giving the hits.

Richards daughter Merrik publicly spoke about an incident her father had told her about as a young girl when she was about 13. He had told her that during his early teen years he was relentlessly bullied by a boy and his friends. These boys would tease Richard every day, they would wait for him outside so they could taunt him or hit him. He found this humiliating, the boy reminded Richard of his father, he had this power over Richard. A power that was fuelled by Richards own fear of him, a power that had Richard running scared from him.

One day Richard told Merrik that he had snapped, he had enough of this boy, he had enough of people laughing at him, hurting him and treating him like a nobody. Angered and upset he had gone into his home, determined not to let this continue. He opened the closet to the coats removing the metal bar that the coats were hung up on and made his way outside.

He sat there alone, angry, hurt, fed up and waited. He waited in silence for this boy to make his usual appearance, he decided that it was time for this boy to get a taste of his own medicine. Sure enough just like clockwork he appeared walking up towards where Richard was sat.

Before the boy could even get his first taunt out of his mouth Richard just started to beat him with the pole. He hit him blow after blow, years of anger came pouring out of the young Kuklinski. All the times he had been teased, hurt and ignored came out in that moment. The pain of his broken relationship with his Father and Mother, the pain of all those years of never feeling good enough, the pain of feeling alone and unwanted. It was all taken out on that boy in one moment of explosive anger

After this release of emotion and pain Richard felt bad about what he had done, but not as much as he thought he would. In some ways he felt good like he had just taken on his demons and beaten them quite literally.

He knew from that day on he wasn't ever going to be a victim again. He wasn't ever going to put up with abuse like he had as a child, and nobody could stop him. That feeling was something he didn't want to lose. It was better to give the abuse not to receive it and he was determined from that point on to be the one dishing it and not taking it.

The only negative aspect of this revenge beating in Richards perception, was the paranoia that he would be caught and punished for what he did. Just as he had with the stolen wine. For weeks he felt like all eyes were on him. It was only a matter of time before the neighbourhood would find out it was him that hurt the boy. This feeling made him restless, he had a sick feeling in his gut. This didn't pass for a while, but when it finally did that feeling of achievement and confidence return.

Richard has spoken about this event on a few occasions since disclosing it with his daughter. He said that the boy he hit was beaten so badly he died. Whether the boy's death is true or not it was a turning point for Richard. It was the moment he transitioned from little Richie the Pollack to Richard Kuklinski, the Iceman, the thief, the killer. The devil himself.

Richard had dropped out of school around the age of 15, instead he would frequent local hang outs or do jobs here and there for local gangs. Sometimes, this would involve stealing and selling on goods for them. He had become very efficient at burglary, he was stealing several things from cars to jewellery.

One of the places he would hang out in between working and doing odd jobs was a local pool hall. Richard loved to play pool and he was incredibly good at the game, getting quite a name for himself as a player. He spent a lot of time learning how to play to pass the hours.

His wife Barbara said he would get a lot of attention when he played, he was in his element, "he was an outstanding pool player and he went to this one particular bar and drew in crowds, and that was his life" – Barbara Kuklinski (2009)

This hobby wasn't always enough to pass the time and he also needed money, he applied for a warehouse job to make a bit of spare cash. After his work shifts ended he would go to the pool hall to play. Richard didn't like being at home so the more things he had to do the better.

During the time Richard had spent at the pool hall he had learned different hustling techniques. He knew he was a good player, around the age of 17 he had begun to hustle visitors passing through. After all, they didn't know how good he was. This would make him a nice little profit. However there came times when his opponents would realise, they were being hustled and confront him about it.

The younger Richard would have run and hid, but then the younger Richard wouldn't have the confidence to try to hustle strangers. But not now, now he didn't care he knew what he was capable of and he was calm, inviting them outside to talk about it. This nonchalant attitude would fade quickly once he had them outside, his impulsive anger would surface, and he would use his pool cue to violently beat them.

By the time he was 18 the change in Richards overall demeanour hadn't gone unnoticed. He caught the eye of the DeCavalcante family, a local New Jersey mafia family. The DeCavalcante's had a number of theft rackets that they ran around New Jersey, they felt that they could profit from Richards skills. They hired him on a few occasions to carry out some car thefts and other robberies for them.

His violent crimes by this point were led by impulsivity and emotive based reactions. Richard was able to make money without using violence or force albeit by conning, stealing and hustling, but nonetheless he did this well and didn't often get caught for it no violence needed. His choice to use violence at this time in his life was reactive, based on how he had interpreted the situation, if he felt insulted or cornered it was his go to behaviour. This made him quite unpredictable at times. He was starting to get a reputation as one not to be messed with.

With these behaviours developing during Richards adolescence, on top of not being caught for them he established a confidence he hadn't had before. One where he was the one in control, one where he was able to have some say over his fate. This behaviour became habit and eventually became part of who he was. The behaviour he had established during his teenage years firmly paved out the criminal career he chose to have in his adult life.

Richard was not the only one from his family to go on to have violent and abusive behaviours. His brother Joseph was brought up in the same environment as Richard was, he witnessed the same types of abuse. This left him with the same ruthless outlook on life. The same volatile mood swings and a twisted set of morals. A man also led by the more primitive reactive emotions such as rage and desire.

These behaviours would control Joseph, he had no handle on them, Richard had somewhat learned how and when to react, he wasn't led by the same types of urges as Joseph was. Richards criminal motives were self-preservation or monetarily driven. Josephs crimes were based around violent sexual control and power.

Joseph went to jail for the rape and murder of a 12-year-old girl. He was in his early 20's at the time he committed this crime. He had snatched the girl and raped her on a roof top. Once he was finished he killed her by throwing her over the roof. The investigation into her murder yielded quick results and Joseph was taken into custody.

He was tried in court and incarcerated in Trenton State Prison the same prison as Richard would later find himself in along-side Joseph. Although Richard said their relationship was estranged and they rarely, if ever, spoke.

3

Adulthood

1956 – 1986

"Assassin? ... that sounds so exotic ...
I was just a murderer"

Richard had moved away from the scared helpless child he had once been. He no longer wanted to be seen as the poor Pollack kid from the projects. Or the boy with weird fitting clothes and a careless family. He would start to be seen as, Rich the guy who took no nonsense, the guy who wouldn't hesitate to harm you, the guy who could get his hands on the things you needed for a low price.

It was 1958 and some of the burglaries Richard had committed were catching up with him. He got arrested with stolen goods in Jersey City and realised it wouldn't be long before the police would look into other robberies and see they might be connected. They would lead back to Richard. The last thing he wanted was to end up in jail, Richard had to decide what to do from here.

This decision became an easy one, when the main men hiring Richard to do burglary jobs went under investigation for organised crimes, Richard knew he needed to lay low. Eventually Richards main sources of income got themselves arrested and sent to jail, the jobs he got offered had started to thin out anyway by this point.

With added pressure of police investigations so close to home it wasn't a wise idea for Richard to keep committing crime, he still needed to make money either way. He decided to get a legitimate job for a while until the heat had cooled off and he could go back to his usual methods of earning. After all a normal 9 to 5 job wouldn't cut it financially for the type of lifestyle Richard wanted.

Richard applied for a job with the Swiftline trucking company in NJ. Not long after he started there, he noticed a beautiful Italian American woman working in the reception, she was about 19 years old and had recently finished high school, her name was Barbara Pedrici.

She got a job as the receptionist at the same warehouse Richard was working in so he would see her daily. Richard decided from the moment he saw her he wanted to be with her. He thought she was beautiful and was determined to date her.

Barbara came from a good family, she was raised by two loving parents who only wanted the best for her. She knew they wouldn't think Richard was the best. Eventually Richard persuaded her to go on a date with him despite her knowing her parents probably wouldn't approve.

When they started dating Barbara didn't want to tell her family that Richard was Polish so she originally said that he was Italian. Her parents had their heart set on her marrying an Italian man. Barbara however was not so interested in that, she just wanted to be with a man that she loved. By that point, the man she loved was Richard.

As things progressed with them Barbara noticed Richard had a bad temper and almost volcanic mood swings going from hot to cold in moments. This scared her, she knew Richard was physically capable of inflicting harm on others just due to his sheer strength and size. He was an intimidating guy even without the violence.

It wouldn't be long before Barbara would get a taste of Richards bad side. As their relationship went on his bad moods would start to appear, he had become controlling. He started to make decisions for Barbara, such as who she could be friends with, when and where she could work. He even attacked Barbara when she tried to leave him.

Emotionally torn and intimidated by Richard, Barbara begun to feel deflated and defeated. She loved this man, he was caring and tried to give her anything she asked for. He would treat her well most of the time and protect her too, but she knew he was no good for her. His moods were scary and unpredictable, there was a very real possibility he could hurt her. Not really knowing how to get away from the situation she had found herself in, she made the decision to stay with him.

They were married in1961 and began a family despite Barbara's initial doubts. By this point Richard was in his mid-20's, he had decided a regular job just wasn't for him. It wasn't long after leaving the trucking company Richard would pick back up old habits and delve back into his life of crime.

Richard had found he needed a regular job, one that he could tell people he did. One that would keep Barbara from asking questions. So, he got work in a film lab via a family member of Barbaras. Initially he was just there to make copies of movies ready for distribution, but Richard being Richard had seen other business opportunities. Such as the ability to bootleg these films and sell them to make a bit of extra cash on the side for himself.

By this point he had begun to steal and con again, this was the only way he felt he could finance the life he wanted for himself and his family. He was doing odd jobs for some of the guys at the film lab he worked in and saw that after hours they had their own bootlegging operation, he wanted in on this. Needing money, he approached a loan shark of the Gambino crime family. After some discussion and once they came to an agreement Richard accepted the loan on offer from them as start-up capital for his bootlegging operation.

Eventually Richard's crimes would begin to progress, he gained more experience in the criminal world. Learning as he went along, he was a quick learner and was happy to try new things. His behaviours and skills altered and adapted to fit the demand there was for jobs, meaning Richard had become multi-talented in crime. This versatility got him attention from all types of criminals, ready to utilise him.

He was hired by the mafia to collect debts as an enforcer and even carried out contract hits for them at times. Richard has claimed he killed many people during this time. He has discussed some of these crimes in documentaries which were televised, and also in books, however he was not convicted for the majority of his claims.

Richard took what he did very seriously, he practiced his crimes and perfected his methods. Over the years it made him very proficient and was a large contribution to the fact he wasn't caught for a very long time.

Richard became known as a criminal freelancer, he would be approached about a variety of things such as the purchase of prescription drugs, car theft, check fraud, weapons & guns, to contract killing. At times he would fulfil these jobs and collect his money, no questions asked. At other times he would con them and kill them. For Richard it didn't matter either way, as long as he wasn't caught, and it paid the amount he needed to maintain his lifestyle, then the victim wasn't his concern.

It was the early 1970's, the Kuklinski family had moved to the suburbs in Durmont New Jersey. Richard was bringing home more money. Some of the jobs he had done for the Gambinos had left him with large amounts of cash ready to be spent. He felt it was time to invest that back into his family. He set up home with Barbara and they settled into the area well.

With his hands in all these pies it was a busy time for Richard, he had to keep up with two lives. The life where he was a hard-working wholesaler, a straight-laced family man, who would work all hours of the day to keep his family in luxury. Then his other life where he was an intimidating enforcer, thief and killer.

He felt confident in his ability to do both but was always paranoid. Paranoid he would be caught, paranoid someone he did business with would talk, paranoid his family would leave him if they found out. This kept him always on edge and alert, in a constant state of what if. Richard knew he had to keep control of everything, there was no way he would let anyone mess up what he had established for himself.

Being a thief, he often needed to get rid of anything he had stolen quickly, to avoid it being traced back to him. He became associated with a man named Phil Solimene, Phil owned a store in Paterson, New Jersey. This store sold a variety of things, including stolen goods. It became a place that criminals would frequent to do deals and arrange sales. People just like Richard and his associates.

You could get most things you needed at the store if you had criminal intent. There would usually be someone there with direct access and if they didn't have what you needed the chances are, they knew someone that did. Richard built a rapport up with the owner Phil over time and would use the store to do some of his dealings, he became well known there.

It was the late 1970's outwardly Richards life was going well. He had a home in the suburbs, a beautiful wife and three adorable children, and a successful wholesale company. He was able to rent nice cars, take his family out and treat them to meals and gifts, his children were attending private schools and his wife didn't have to work. By all accounts it seemed to anyone on the outside that Richard was living the American dream.

Far from his sorry beginnings in the projects, he had turned full throttle and moved completely away from the life little Richie had led.

During this period Richard met Percy House, Gary Smith and Daniel Deppner. The men together were a force to be reckoned with, they specialised in car theft, robbery and fraud.

They worked together on many occasions and eventually formed a Burglary gang. This gang was organised and efficient, the two ring leaders were Richard and Percy and the others would work under their instruction.

Percy House was not the kind of man who could be trusted, he was a crook through and through, and just like Richard he did whatever it took to save his own skin. Richard saw these characteristics in him and kept him at arm's length. That said, Percy was good at what he did so for the gang was somewhat of an asset.

Richards burglary gang earned quite a reputation for themselves, they were working freelance so would take on jobs for all types of people. Word got around about them, and with this criminal popularity came criminal investigation. There had been a spike in Robberies in certain areas and the police were on the lookout for the people responsible.

He learned early on as a man to keep your cards close to your chest and friends at arm's length. Afterall he couldn't be trusted so how could he trust them. So far, all life had taught him was that most people will either hurt you, con you, leave you or torment you. He also knew there were people capable of doing all of those things, and the best thing to do was have the upper hand at all times. If his own parents couldn't do him right, then a stranger most definitely cannot be trusted.

Although Richard had worked with his gang on many jobs he hadn't got too close to any of them. He still kept them within arm's reach, creating a false sense of security that implied friendship. He knew if the time ever came, he may need to get rid of them, so he maintained a façade of the loyal associate. They could take him down if they ever talked to the police, anyone he did business with could. This was something always in the back of Richards mind, it nagged at him all the time.

Due to this mistrust Richard kept his circle of associates small, he had a few people he would consider as working friends. Anyone outside of this circle was irrelevant and didn't matter.

Richard had a couple of associates outside of his burglary gang and Phil at the store. He would do business with them regularly. One of these people was George Malliband, they both dealt in the distribution of stolen goods and would also sell bootleg copies of pornography. Over the years George and Richard worked together multiple times and became used to each other's company.

Another person he met was a man called Robert Prongay, Richard and Robert would discuss and plan crimes together. Robert was a person who had knowledge on things such as chemicals, explosives, and military based training. Richard found his knowledge especially useful and would talk to him about ideas he had for contract murders and cons he had set up. Robert had told Richard he was also being hired as a hitman and one of the reasons he knew so much about killing people was because he was doing it himself.

They shared stories and ideas often, Robert wasn't shy of committing crime or just helping out others with their crimes if the price was right. Just like Richard, Robert Prongay lived a double life. To outsiders he was Mister Softee the harmless ice-cream man, but to criminals like Richard he was an educated contract killer. Just like Richard, Robert tormented his family with violent outbursts and threats. The two men had much in common.

According to Richards claims they used Robert's ice cream freezer he kept in his garage to store a body. Partly to cover a murder and partly as an experiment to see if they could distort time of death and botch any investigation into the murder. A good example of their working relationship.

Richard had become an established career criminal; he was adept at this lifestyle and seemingly comfortable in it. Becoming somewhat arrogant at his own ability, his confidence grew as did his ability to put absolute fear into anyone. He would start to become complacent and careless in his crimes, but too confident to care if it may leave a path back to him.

His empire would soon come crumbling down bit by bit. With bodies showing up and associates being arrested the beginning of the end was coming for Richard Kuklinski.

4

Jekyll and Hyde

Good Richie and Bad Richie

1960 - 1986

"I've never felt sorry for anything I've done.
Other than hurting my family."

Richard's ability to live two separate lives was helped by the fact his wife and children would not question his day-to-day habits or work routine. Barbara stated that if he got up in the middle of the night and left the house she would never question it or bring it up looking for a reason. This was something she learned to do early on in their marriage.

She had an inkling that he was up to no good at times but never really knew exactly what it was he was doing. For the most part she was under the impression he worked in distribution and dealt with goods at wholesale prices, which he sold in bulk. At times Richard would come home with large sums of cash and he would treat the family. Barbara was told the money came from deals and sales he had made through his company.

While he was working at the film lab he was doing a mixture of legitimate and illegitimate work. Barbara didn't know he had been making bootleg copies of things on the side such as the pornography. Many of these types of things she wasn't aware of until he was arrested in 1986.

Even the moments where she could plainly see the police had Richard under surveillance, she had no real idea why they were watching him. At points in time she felt the whole operation into him was pointless because Richard knew they were watching him. He would leave hours early for meetings just to scope the meeting areas out first to see who had followed him. She couldn't envision them catching him out on anything.

Barbara didn't see the point in asking questions about it all. It would only make him angry and it would cause an argument. He didn't like the police, he had no time or respect for them. Barbara knew better than to talk about things that Richard had no time for.

Barbara was herself, a victim of abuse at the hands of Richard. This began early on in their relationship. She describes him as being two different people, much like Jekyll and Hyde, "there's the good Richie, then there's the bad Richie" - Barbara Kuklinski (1992).

After dating Richard for some time and getting moments of his mad rages, bad moods and vicious mouth Barbara had decided it wasn't working out. She felt intimidated by him and often worried about how he might react to things.

He had become controlling, she no longer worked at her receptionist job because Richard didn't want her working there. He had insisted that she quit, at first she was resistant and told him she didn't want to. Barbara enjoyed her job, why should she quit? But he had worn her down, she eventually gave into his demands and left.

This wasn't an isolated incident, Richard had also tried to put a stop to Barbara seeing some of her friends. He would try to tell her who she could and couldn't be friends with and who she could talk to.

This wasn't what she wanted, she cared about Richard but didn't want to put up with some of the behaviours he was showing her. Barbara decided it was time to call it off and have a break from Richard.

She arranged to meet up with him to tell him that she needed some time alone and wanted him to start seeing other people. Richard didn't take this news well, his reaction was one of pure anger. She had seen him mad before but not like this. There was a look on his face, one she hadn't seen before. Instant dread started to seep from her head slowly down her body, in that moment she realised she didn't know what he was going to do.

Completely shocked, Barbara sees Richards arm moving closer towards her and she feels something sharp against her back. She reaches round to grab where she feels the pain and there's blood. Richard pulled back his arm, at this moment Barbara sees a knife in his hand. She realises he had stabbed her and starts to scream in panic. In this moment Richard said to Barbara, "don't you ever try to leave me"

Luckily the damage Richard had done with the knife was superficial and Barbara although hurt and shaken up was physically okay. But the damage he caused to Barbara that day emotionally and psychologically was serious. Within a day of this happening Richard had shown up begging her to take him back, when she refused the bad Richard came back out.

He said to her very confidently if you don't get back with me Barbara, I will kill you. If I can't have you, then nobody can.

This scared Barbara, she agreed to get back together with him. In that moment it seemed like her safest option. Richard was possibly capable of anything. She didn't want to take the chance and not believe him and refuse only for him to kill her and maybe even her family.

Barbara had seen how people were scared of Richard. She had noticed that no one seemed to question him, or ever confront him. This was how Richard liked it, of course he didn't want to be questioned or challenged. To him this was a sign of respect, Richard equates fear with respect.

Barbara didn't see respect she saw a problem, one that she cannot get away from. She knew leaving him wasn't the safe option for her at that time.

They got married on September 8th, 1961, shortly after all of this happened, this was a rushed marriage by Richard, he wanted to solidify their relationship. So marriage and children are what he wanted next. After the wedding they moved in together, to begin their new life as the Kuklinski's.

Richard had promised Barbara that he would look after her. That he would make sure she lived comfortably no matter what it took.

Soon after they got married Barbara fell pregnant with their eldest daughter, and from the outside life seemed to be going pretty well for the newlyweds. Richard had made himself seem like a real family man to those that knew him. He had started up a company and went by the job title of wholesale distributor.

After having 3 children together, 2 girls and 1 boy they needed a bigger home. Richard had money coming in and decided it was time for them to move. The house they moved to was in a popular suburban area of Dumont in New Jersey, with nice parks, good local shops and great schools. By all accounts it was exactly what Barbara had wanted.

The rest of the world would only get a view of the good Richard when it came to his image with his family. He would rent nice cars and take his family out on trips or for meals. He would buy them extravagant gifts. He felt there wasn't anything he wouldn't do to keep his family without financial strife. He didn't want them to go without like he had to. He would keep his other life separated from them, telling his children he worked in wholesale distribution and sold things like clothes.

Richards children, however, explain it wasn't all smiles and outings like their father would have people believe. They recall times of sheer terror when Richard lost his temper, he would get depressed for days and become irritable, then just explode. He would break things around the home, shout, hit things and also hit Barbara. His daughters and son were witness to this violence on multiple occasions.

In a televised interview one of his daughters talks about him threatening their life. Richard sat her down one day and told her, "Merri if it goes too far, and I ever Kill your Mom, that I would have to kill all of you" - Merrik Kuklinski (2019) Richard did this when his daughter was only 13, after seeing his rages and knowing he was unpredictable she wouldn't argue with him.

His eldest daughter Kristen attempted to stop him hitting her mother. She stood between them, but it didn't work. She was so small in comparison to her father, he would just pick her up and move her out of the way. The children felt they had no power to stop what was happening. This feeling of powerlessness has impacted them their whole lives.

Over the years Barbara started to recognise tell-tale signs of Richards mood, she could almost predict if he was in a good mood or a bad one just from the atmosphere he brought into the room.

This was not something she was always able to do, in Anthony Bruno's book it is explained that there were times his outbursts had seemed to come out of nowhere. That he could be angry about something for weeks and keep it hidden so well she would have no idea about it until one of his rages happened.

Money can be earned no matter who you are in life, but love is something that is learned. If a person is never taught to love and only raised with examples of hate, then they themselves won't have developed the social skills and habits to love people in a healthy way.

Richard wasn't shown how a loving family behaves, he wasn't nurtured during his childhood. He was in a constant state of survival, one where he was never sure what would happen next. One where he never had any real pleasure in life other than ones, he had created in moments for himself. He was often forgotten about and was witness and victim to violence.

It's almost as if Richard wishes his family were objects he could control. That he can dress up and pose to portray the family he depicts in his mind as perfect. Even if those captured moments are a lie it doesn't matter. It all reinforces Richards Ideals and keeps him removed from the memories of his childhood, conning himself that he is giving his own children better. When in fact these things he detested as a child have manifested in his own behaviours. He was making his children victims of the same things he was as a boy, the things he despised his own father for he had become himself.

Richard exposed his family to the same behaviour he resented his own parents for. He repeated the cycle of abuse, his own wife and children suffering the things that damaged him as a child. Yet he expected them not to react to it, to just accept that this is how it is. His own needs prioritising over the hurt he was causing to others, all that mattered to him in those moments was his feelings.

On the other side of his personality, there was good Richie. A loving caring man who wanted nothing more than to spoil his wife and children. A man who would do anything to satisfy their every wish. He would shower Barbara with affection and gifts. Buy his children unnecessary, but lavish presents. Often, he would take the family out to expensive restaurants or on family outings.

There are times Barbara has spoken of him fondly, she speaks of the Richard she fell in love with, not the bad Richie but the good Richie. When she speaks of first meeting him she thought he was so handsome and intriguing. "Richard was very good looking, I mean I did notice him on the platform. You know tall, slim, very good looking and interesting" – Barbara Kuklinski (2009)

He wooed her with flowers and compliments, he was kind and considerate, respectful and hardworking, he was the Richie she loved

The one that went above and beyond on family occasions, the one who told her she was the most beautiful woman alive, the Richie who would get up at night and tend to the babies so she could get more sleep. The man she would walk hand in hand with like they had no worries in the world, take trips to feed the ducks and just spend some peaceful time alone together.

There was a side of Richard that would try to be a good father and husband, a side so desperate to be the only thing that mattered to his children and wife, their superhero. Like a father should be. Not like his father, it was the furthest thing away from what Stanley was.

It seemed this part of Richard craved what he saw as the perfect family, the family he never got to have growing up. The family he always wanted to have, and to be the father he never experienced. He was so focused on creating this perfect little bubble that when he would have an outburst, he would feel guilt at the way he had treated them and try to correct his mistakes as soon as possible.

It was as if Richard felt that these superficial things such as expensive cars, posed family pictures and meals were the core of a happy family and were something that showed the rest of the world they were a perfect family. The hope that these spoils would cancel out any other behaviour he had done behind closed doors. He knew deep down the damage he was doing to them but tried to ignore it, so he didn't have to face the fact that he was just like Anna and Stanley.

For decades, his family walked around on eggshells never quite sure who they would be getting that day.

A constant limbo of wondering if it was a good Richie or bad Richie kind of day.

5

Links to the Mafia

1953 – 1986

"It was due to business"
Kuklinski explaining in court why he killed

Richard has had a long history of working on and off as a freelancer for the Mafia. According to police testimony this began around 1953 when Richard was about the age of 18.

By this point his thieving ways had got him noticed by the DeCavalcante family. They saw how efficient he was at getting his hands-on stolen goods and felt as though he could profit from this. He formed the Breaking and entering gang and did freelance jobs for them.

Richard had also had cash loans from the mafia on different occasions, not all of these transactions went smoothly, however he paid back what he owed each time. His relationship with them overall hasn't been a smooth one, but none the less over the years Richard has had multiple dealings with them.

Eventually these connections with families such as the DeCavalcante's and the Gambino's would lead him to other jobs, like car theft, commercial robbery and ultimately murder for hire.

Early in the 1950's he began working as a freelance thief for the DeCavalante family, but the work started to die down in 1960 so he got a legitimate job to help finance his life. The working relationship with the DeCavalcantes ceased for a while and he got legitimate work.

Eventually he left the trucking company he was working for, shortly after he married Barbara. After this he was looking for more work, he found it in film production and distribution, thus began his bootlegging career.

Kuklinski had got this job via his wife's uncle. This is where Richard would eventually make bootleg porn. Deluxe Films was a film lab Richard worked in which was owned by Robert DiBernardo. DiBernardo was also a member of a crime family and was well known for his role in the production and distribution of pornography.

Originally Richard had worked for the film lab producing legitimate films for distribution, all above board and legally. He had wanted to make a bit of extra cash on the side, so started to make bootleg copies of the films. He had access to master copies of popular films by companies such as Disney. He would then sell them on at a lower price.

Over time Richard noticed that adult films sold much more quickly and in higher quantities. He realised he could make more money bootlegging these films compared to others. He wanted to expand his operation but didn't have the cash flow for it. This was when he approached the Gambino family and asked for a loan to start up the side hustle.

After an agreement was made Richard was able to start producing these films for resale in larger quantities which meant more money. However, Richard had not lined up buyers for the material and without buyers there is no money. This meant that he had to work on getting sales. He now owed $65,000 to the Gambino family and they would be coming to collect for payments soon.

He started to fall behind on payments due to distribution problems. Late one evening while he was making copies, he had a visit. As he was finishing up for the night, making his way to leave, the lift door opened, and out came three enforcers for the Gambino's. They started to demand the money he owed on a late payment; money Richard didn't have. Surrounding him as they came out of the lift, they ushered him into the restroom.

As he stepped in the room his knee was kicked out from under him, he fell to the floor. A crashing blow suddenly impacted the back of his head, finding it hard to focus he told them he would get them the payment. By this point he had been hit across the head again and kicked in the ribs a few times.

Winded but ok he said he would get their money by Friday. They were not satisfied with this reply and demanded the whole debt to be paid. Richard agreed to pay the whole amount by that Friday, by that point he just wanted them to leave. He could figure out a game plan once they had gone.

Before they left the largest out of the three men yelled back at Richard, "Now don't you forget Pollack" – Bruno (1993) Richard later found out this man was Roy DeMeo. This was his initial introduction to Roy. A person up until then Richard had only heard about.

It was alleged by Kuklinski, not long after this introduction to Roy DeMeo that he began to work as a hitman regularly for the Gambino family, specifically for Roy DeMeo. However, this has not been completely verified. Roy DeMeo was involved in the contracted deaths of many people. The DeMeo crew would liaise at a place called the Gemini lounge in Brooklyn and it was here that they allegedly would treat the bodies of the victims for disposal.

Although some dispute Richard even doing any kind of dealing with the Gambino's, there is other evidence, he did have affiliation to them. Even if only briefly in passing business deals.

He was photographed outside the Gemini lounge during police surveillance. This happened at least one time, showing that he had visited the lounge. However, there is only one image of him, and it was stated that on this specific occasion he went there to purchase a handgun, not because he was directly working for DeMeo. Nonetheless it does verify that he did indeed have some connection to the crime family.

Richard would frequent a novelty store in Paterson New Jersey, known by the locals as only 'the Paterson store' or "the store" – Supplementary report (1988). It was owned by a man named Phil Solimene who was known to be involved with many shady dealings. The store was a place that many criminals would frequent to carry out activities such as arranging deals, trading and exchanging stolen goods. This store was used by mafia members and associates from time to time too.

Richard was seen talking to associates and mafia members at the store on multiple occasions. This was observed whilst he was under surveillance and during the undercover operation carried out by the ATF and the New Jersey state police into Kuklinski. Over time they had gathered evidence of his affiliation to these people. Then used this affiliation to get access to him for their sting.

Using this knowledge of his connections the undercover operation 'Iceman' successfully made initial contact with Richard via the informants they had at the store. One of these informants was Phil Solimene the store owner.

This meant Dominick Polifrone was then able to initiate a working relationship with Richard. Dominick knew that people knew of 'big Rich' and knew he was in the business of making money no questions asked, even if it meant murder. Him being introduced to Richard via people such as Phil Solimene was vital to the case.

It also highlights that Richard did have such connections, the types of connections that lead to the contracted murder of others. One such contract is that of Peter Calabro.

Calabro was a crooked officer who had information on a car theft ring operated by the crime family. The Gambinos were worried he would flip, inform on them and take a witness protection plea deal. So they wanted him killed before he could expose them. It is alleged that they hired Richard Kuklinski to do this.

Peter Calabro was murdered by Richard. According to Richard it was a hired hit organised by the Gambino family which he executed for a fee. Peter Calabro's body was found March 14th, 1980 on the side of a road with two shotgun wounds being the cause of his death. When he was found he was still inside his car. According to Richard, Sammy 'the Bull' Gravano was supposedly the one to arrange it. That is however disputed.

The evidence that the police had on this hit wasn't enough to stand alone in court as definitive proof that it was set up by the Gambinos. Richard's statement, however, included information that was never released to the public, which supported the evidence that law enforcement already had about the case. With the inclusion of the confession Kuklinski had made, it meant they had enough to make a conviction against Sammy Gravano. After Richard pled guilty and was convicted of the murder of Calabro, he was asked to stand up in court and testify against Sammy, which he agreed to do, but this time would never come.

New Jersey prosecutors were forced to drop all charges against Sammy for the death of Calabro, after Kuklinski's untimely death. This is where the suspicions over Kuklinski's death come from. Some suspect his death was down to slow poisoning over time rather than natural causes. Allegedly this was done to stop him testifying against Sammy the Bull. However, others state his death was of natural causes and there was no foul play on the part of Sammy.

It wasn't unusual for the mafia to outsource or work with those outside of the mafia, that included organising murder. A brief look into the mafias history gives some examples of this. During the 1930's the Sicilian and Italian mafia families broke away from their rooted traditions. They formed Cosa Nostra, which was similar in its beliefs but different in structure. The tolerance of working with those outside of the families became more lenient.

This meant people such as Lucky Lucciano would openly work and do business with men such as Meyer Lansky and Bugsy Siegel. During the 1930's onward they would often work with Jewish mobsters. Murder Inc are an example of Jewish mobsters carrying out hits for Italian Mafia members.

During the 1970's and 80's the Russian mafia had business ties with the Genovese and Colombo families in a well-known gasoline tax evasion scheme. Master minded by Michael Franzese where the Government lost millions in tax.

These documented cases provide examples of Italian Mafia families working with those outside of the Italian mafia, in serious crimes. Of course, this does not mean they would discuss the dealings or inside knowledge of Cosa Nostra, but if there was money to be made or debts to be settled, they could overlook a person's heritage.

It isn't so hard to believe given Richards other connections with the Gambino and DeCavalcante families that he was offered differing jobs with them. Richard was an ask no questions type of guy, exactly the type of person mafia members and associates like to work with. As long as Richard got his money, that was all that mattered, he wasn't interested in the reason or rhyme behind the job.

There are social aspects of having an association to the mafia, which Richard would view to be beneficial to him, such as the identity status it could bring. These would increase his motivation to be connected to them on more than just a monetary basis.

For Richard it would have been a good opportunity career wise to be associated with the mafia. The reputation of the mafia is one of control, fear and wealth, things Richard desired greatly. Richard refused to be seen as the weak one, or as a victim.

Being associated with people like the Gambino family would mean strength, control, and respect. For Richard no task would have been too small or big to achieve this connection to them. Getting involved with them would not only pay the bills but also inflate his self-worth and alter his social status within the criminal world, giving him the identity, he craved.

He enjoyed the lifestyle that came with the pay checks and the association to them, it was a life he never had growing up. His determination to financially maintain this lifestyle and continue to do jobs for them meant he was willing to go to extremes to keep that association going.

Richard has also used this mafia connection to make some bold claims, claims he knew were farfetched and false. Due to this it can be difficult to believe that he had a connection to them at all, which has left many labelling him as a liar, despite there being documented evidence of his affiliation to them.

Over the years leading up to his death Richard made many claims to murders of some notorious mafia members. Men such as Jimmy Hoffa, Paul Castellano and Carmine Galante.

He shared elaborate stories of these murders often getting information about the crime scene wrong, in other cases contradicting the testimony of many witnesses. Such claims can be quickly disproven when looking at crime scene photos or reading reports on the investigations.

Richard even claimed responsibility for the murder of Roy DeMeo, he said it was over the situation between him and soon to be victim George Malliband. However, New York police records suggest the evidence of the case didn't fit Kuklinski's account and that they had on good sources the death of DeMeo was ordered by Paul Castellano and it was Nino Gaggi who arranged it. It had nothing to do with Kuklinski.

So, although Richard can be tied to the mafia there is no clear link that he was a regular hitman for them. There is evidence he would do business with them and has carried out murder for them. But the frequency of this remains unclear. It can be said with some certainty that not all of Richards mafia stories are true and are more tall tales with some truthful ones thrown into the mix.

Victims

Richard has claimed multiple victims during his criminal career. Many of these were admissions to contract kills he carried out, supposedly on behalf of the mafia and other criminal associates.

These will not all be discussed in this section unless there is some basis to them that can be linked to verifiable evidence.

The main cases discussed will be the 5 murders he was convicted for during the late 1980's. This includes the case of Paul Hoffman, for which charges were dropped in return for a confession to the murders of George Malliband and Louis Masgay.

Two other murder cases will be discussed, both are technically unsolved due to no person being named as responsible for them by authorities. These two cases are the case of Bar owner Bruno Latini, an associate of Richards and a Mr Robert Prongay, a man Richard knew and claimed he worked with from the late 1970's into the early 1980's.

6

Bruno Latini

December 24th, 1971

During a filmed and televised interview in 2001 Richard discussed killing a man in the early hours of the morning on Christmas Eve. This man was identified by Richard as Bruno Latini.

Bruno Latini was from New York he lived in the Bronx and he owned a bar in the heart of Manhattan. Bruno was a well-known guy in his local area, having a bar meant he was a familiar face to his regular custom. He had grown up in New York, so it was home for him.

Despite being a legitimate business owner Bruno did have some criminal associates namely mafia associates. It was rumoured he did business with them regularly. However, he was not a known criminal, at least not to the police. His records show that he had only been arrested once and this was for a DUI, but other than that, there was nothing that would link him to crime on record.

According to Richards claims Bruno Latini had owed Richard money, about $1600 in total, money which he could do with so close to Christmas.

Richard describes being at home with his family on the night of December 23rd and being distracted by the nagging thoughts of this debt. The whole evening this was on his mind, he couldn't concentrate on Barbara and the kids while this was occupying his thoughts.

Once everyone had gone to bed Richard tried to relax but couldn't. He felt like the guy was taking liberties, and no one took liberties with Richard. The more he thought about it the angrier he became. He decided he had to act then and there, he wanted that money, the guy was overdue a visit anyway.

Richard got up grabbing his keys and his jacket and headed to the door with purpose. He got into his car and began to drive, stopping off to contact the man to tell him they needed to meet. After making arrangements with Bruno he headed to Manhattan, this drive took about an hour, plenty of time for Richard to stew in his thoughts.

According to Richard they met in a quiet area in a parking lot during the early hours of the morning, on the 24th of December 1971. Richard parked his car and made his way over to Bruno's car and got into the passenger's seat.

Richard confronted Bruno about the money he was owed. To which Bruno replied that he didn't have the money to pay Richard off, but he had some cash on him if Richard wanted to go for a drink to celebrate Christmas.

Not satisfied with Bruno's answer Richard, declined his offer and said that he only came for the money he was owed. Without hesitation Richard shot him three times in the head inside the car. Richard describes the event as disorienting. Unloading the gun in such a confined space was very loud and the flash that was created by the gun impaired his vision and stunned him momentarily.

He then got his bearings and waited a few minutes for his eyesight to come back before making his way back to his car. He then drove back home.

Richards claims to this murder have come into question based on some inconsistencies with his events and evidence found at the crime scene.

It's not out of the ordinary for Richard to kill a man over money, Richard prioritised money over taking a life. Money was extremely important to Richard. Which is why his victims were never found with cash on them because Richard would take it.

Richard claimed that Bruno Latini owed him $1600 however, police and news reports showed that Latini's body was found with "$500 in $10 bills" - NY Times (1971) which was discovered by the police in Mr. Latini's wallet along with expensive Jewellery that he was wearing and a collection of about "two dozen loose keys" - NY Times (1971) in his pocket. An unopened gift and a .38 Caliber handgun were also found in the car. The gun was registered to the victim and was not the gun used to kill him. There was no evidence to suggest that the murder was motivated by money or that it was a robbery.

Based on Richards known behaviours in these types of crimes, for him to leave a large sum of money at the crime scene was unheard of. It definitely doesn't fit with regular patterns of behaviour Richard had established during other similar crimes.

There is only one similarity in this crime which fits Richards M.O. but would not be enough to suggest that Richard was the one responsible. That similarity was the murder weapon and the way in which Bruno was killed. Bruno Latini was found in his car with 3 bullet wounds to the head which were determined as the cause of death.

He was shot with a .38 Caliber, this was the same type of gun Richard used, however, .38 is a popular gun many people own them and use them. So, this wouldn't be definitive proof that it was Richard who carried out this shooting.

The crime scene itself was indicative of a mafia style hit, although at the time police had indicated they had no evidence to suggest it was linked to organised crime. That said, the murder was carried out in a car park, in a public area, the body was left where it lay, no items were stolen from the car or the victim. This would indicate a typical mafia execution styled hit rather than a murder over money.

This killing also occurred during a time there was tension in the world of the mafia. During 1971 a number of mafia members and associates had shown up dead in very similar circumstances to that of Bruno. Almost 6 months after Latini's death it was published by the New York Times that Bruno Latini among 14 others were victims that had been linked to a string of mafia associated hits. His death was put on record as a mafia hit with the shooter remaining un-named, rather than being recorded as a murder over the money.

7

George Malliband

1st February 1980

"I shot George Malliband 5 times"
Kuklinski 1988 in court admitting to the
murder of his friend and business
associate.

George Malliband was a stocky man with a heavy-set frame, he had dark hair, and favoured a large well-kept moustache and often wore large dark glasses.

He grew up in Huntington Pennsylvania and attended Huntingdon Area High school during the 1950's.

He had two younger siblings Ronald and Donald who were twins, they lived with both parents growing up and by all accounts were just your regular family.

George came from a family that had good business ethics. His father owned companies in Huntingdon which were what he dedicated his life to. This work ethic was passed onto his children. They all had a keen interest in owning and running companies and seemed to do a good job at it.

The family suffered two deaths during the late 60's and early 70's. A tragic time for all of them.

On November 5th, 1968 Georges brother Ronald was driving on route 22, PA when he had an unfortunate car crash which killed him, he suffered severe head injuries. The crash was in the newspaper due to Ronald being a successful businessman, the loss was felt by the community. The article reads "A young Huntingdon businessman Ronald E Malliband 28 of 644 Fifth Street was instantly killed early today when his sports car crashed on the Long Hollow near McVeytown. Malliband a partner with his twin brother Donald in the Interstate Aluminium Company of Huntingdon suffered severe head injuries." – Huntingdon daily news (11.05/1968)

A few years later in 1971 George also lost his mother, she was only 59 at the time. These kinds of losses to a family are devastating and surely impacted Georges choices over the years that proceeded their deaths.

When it came to gambling George was hooked, he spent a lot of his time and money on it. It was a bad habit he couldn't shake and eventually it got him into serious debts. Debts with the wrong kinds of people. George had resorted to borrowing money from loan sharks to try to clear his debts, but it had made his situation worse when he started falling behind on his payments.

He couldn't afford the mounting interest on each loan he owed money to. He was finding it harder and harder to keep each person at bay, soon word got around about his failure to repay some of these debts. He was getting a bit of a reputation as an unreliable gambling addict, something that later on would contribute to his brutal fate.

George Malliband was an acquaintance of Richards, they had done business on and off for about 5 years. George dealt in the production and distribution of bootleg pornography and stolen goods among other things and was a person Richard regularly spent time with.

As with any of his business associates, Richard would keep them separated from his home life. However, George, unlike others had been to Kuklinski's family home on one occasion. Richard had stated that he had briefly bought George to his home mainly out of politeness to give George a sense of acceptance. But that it was something he had regretted doing ever since.

Richard on the whole didn't have any issues with George. They did business and then went their separate ways in-between deals. This all changed after George unknowingly made his first mistake.

One afternoon during the late 70's Richard and Barbara were holding a cookout for their daughter's birthday. This was a small gathering of close family and friends, invite only. During the day's festivities George had shown up at Richards home. Richard was furious at this but didn't want to ruin the day for his daughter by loosing his temper with George, so he gritted his teeth and allowed him to stay for a little while.

The whole time George was there Richard was seething, he just couldn't believe the audacity of the guy, thinking it was okay to come to a personal family gathering un-invited. How dare he do that; he wasn't anyone important enough to Richard to warrant an invitation into Richards personal world. George was not a man Richard wanted his family being exposed to. This was something Richard would never forget or let go. If anyone could hold a grudge it was him, especially if it involved his family.

After that day Richard had tried to put the event to the back of his mind, he thought it was his own fault that George knew where to go to find Richards home. After all he was the one who initially showed him where it was. He carried on doing business with George despite this building annoyance.

About a year before George was murdered, he had gone into business with Richard officially. The business was in the reproduction and sale of pornographic films. It was based out of Richards office and was under the name The Sunset Company, located in Dumont in New Jersey.

While working together they had been doing distribution deals with Roy DeMeo's crew. During this time George had needed financial help and had asked DeMeo for a loan.

Roy refused to loan him the money as there was no guarantee that George could pay it back, so Richard had agreed to vouch for him. He told DeMeo not to worry that George was good for the money and that he would make sure George kept up with the payments.

Roy eventually agreed to loan George the money, on the condition that he was holding them both responsible for it. If George fell behind on his payments, then Roy would contact Richard as well as George.

George was still gambling despite his mounting debts, he owed casinos and loan sharks who he was ducking and diving. He had not paid much of what he owed, the pressure on him was increasing. George had started to panic; he had no idea how he was going to repay all these people. It wasn't long before word got round to the DeMeo crew that George was coming up short on other debts. They started to ask around to find out who he owed money to, when Roy found out that George owed significant amounts of money he'd had enough. He wanted his money, there was no way George was going to wriggle out of this one.

Roy contacted Richard and told him to bring George to see him in New York, he told Richard he wanted his money. As he saw Richard as partly responsible, he wanted them both at the meeting to hear what he had to say.

According to Richards Police Statement he met up with George on the 29th of January 1980 after George had called him the previous day and told Richard to pick him up from his home in Huntingdon. They went out for food and drinks around 6-7pm to discuss the trip to see Roy and then both men made their way back. George went home and Richard stayed in a local motel.

Police reports identified a number of bank transactions that were carried out on the 29th for large sums of money. This was only days before George disappeared.

Earlier in the day on the 29th George had gone to the bank to pay in two checks from his account that Richard had given him previously. One for the sum of $4,000 and the other for the sum of $3,500. Both checks were under the payee name of Sunset Company which was Richards company. According to Richard this was money he had owed George and he was just paying some of it back to him.

Witnesses also stated in police reports they saw George with Kuklinski in the driveway of Georges home only days before he disappeared. They reported to the police that when they had spoken to George on the same day George had told them he had $27,000 in cash and was worried that something might happen to him. He wouldn't explain why he thought that, but just expressed his concerns to them.

When Richard was questioned about the cash George had on him that day, he denied knowing how much was there but admitted knowing George had cash, and alleged it was something George did sometimes. He had known him to carry thousands of dollars at times.

The next day January 30th Richard called George around 8am and said he was on the way to get him. They would go for some breakfast and discuss the day and get the plan into action to get DeMeos money.

According to Investigation reports for about 2 days (31st Jan & 1st Feb) George said on at least 3 separate occasions to people he knew, that he was worried about something and mentioned that he thought something bad might happen to him.

People George had spoken to reported him sounding paranoid on the telephone and in person but said he wouldn't elaborate on what he was worried about. The last time he spoke to anyone other than Richard was via phone and he had said he was in the office of Richard Kuklinski.

Shortly before George went missing he checked into the Holiday Inn, Bergen New Jersey not far from Richards office and home. He arrived on the 31st Jan 1980 at 11.56pm and signed for his key. This was the last known location where George was seen alive. It is on the Holiday Inn records that he checked out before 12 noon on the 1st of Feb 1980 but after that his whereabouts remain questionable.

After the last call George made around 1pm on the 1st of Feb from Richards office it is not really known what happened. According to Richard they had made their way to the meeting with DeMeo. Roy confronted George about all the money he owed to different people. He said he could no longer trust him to repay his debts because he had heard he was letting other people down.

Roy demanded that Georges debt be repaid in full. He told them that he was giving them 3-4 days to come up with the cash or there would be dire consequences.
At the meeting Richard was told clearly that he would meet the same fate as George if George didn't pay. Roy allegedly asked Richard why he would vouch for George if George had a gambling problem. To which Richard claimed he knew nothing about a gambling problem and that when he vouched for George he knew George was good for the money.

It is said that it was on the drive back from this meeting that triggered the disagreement between Richard and George which resulted in George being shot.

During the drive back to Bergen in a panic George had demanded the money Richard owed him to pay the debt he had with DeMeo. When Richard refused George told Richard he had to help him get the money another way. Richard asked George, what if I don't help? George replied with, I know where you live Rich.

Kuklinski knew George knew where his family lived, he saw this as a direct threat towards his family. That day George had shown up at the cookout instantly returned to Richards mind. The immediate anger and disgust came rushing to the forefront of his thoughts. Suddenly Richard was thinking what if this guy tells DeMeo where my family is. He feels at this moment he has no other choice but to get rid of George. Richards family was far too important to put at risk.

Within moments Richard had stopped the vehicle pulling up on a roadside. The conversation had gone silent by this point. George realising that Richard wasn't happy had trailed off his moaning and awkwardly sat there as the van slowed up. Richard turned towards George, gun in hand and did not hesitate.

He shot George in the chest numerous times, George was killed instantly. Richard stole the cash George had on his persons, which was rumoured to be roughly between 25 and 27 thousand dollars.

Richard then disposed of his body by putting it into a metal 55-gallon barrel which he then dumped over the edge of a cliff near a chemical plant in New Jersey.

Malliband like Richard was a large man, Richard struggled to get him into the metal barrel. To combat this Richard had cut the tendons in Georges legs and arms so he could bend his body into the barrel. It had been a tight squeeze, because of this when Richard had rolled the barrel off the side of a cliff edge it had popped open exposing some of Georges hacked leg. His body was found 3 days later by an employee of the plant who had noticed the leg sticking out of the barrel and gone to investigate it.

After speaking with George's family members, they learned that George had said he was going that day to meet a Richard Kuklinski whom he had business with. Multiple people had identified that George was last seen with Richard. Generally Richards style wasn't generally committing unplanned crimes.

One of the biggest reasons he wasn't caught for many of his crimes was because he thought his crimes through and planned them out step by step. This was how he ensured he avoided things such as being easily detected by witnesses. This time though his emotions had got the better of him and he had killed George on impulse not really thinking about the trail leading back to him.

This impulsivity would be one of the biggest mistakes Richard would make and was a mistake that helped to identify him, getting convictions against him.

8

Peter Calabro

March 14th, 1980

Peter Calabro wasn't associated to Richard Kuklinski directly but in many ways, they had plenty in common. He was a victim of Richards at the hands of a shotgun and was associated with the same members of the Gambino family that Richard was. Peter was 36 when he was killed, he was married, owned a home and worked a full-time job.

Peter Calabro was a police officer, he started working for the NYPD in 1970. He worked for the auto-theft unit and had been with the department nearly ten years. A colleague and long-time friend John Doherty was someone he worked alongside. Their job was to help gather intelligence on auto theft crimes, make arrests and investigate potential crimes related to the theft of cars.

But little did the rest of the department know that Peter was a crooked cop, he had been secretly working for a number of car theft gangs around New York and New Jersey. He would turn a blind eye to crimes for a fee or give the gangs inside information at a cost. By the mid 70's his links to organised crime had expanded after meeting some influential people in the auto theft world.

Peters colleague John had introduced him to a man named Roy DeMeo. John had known Roy a while and had personal connections to him. John's brother Daniel was working as a bartender in a place called The Gemini Lounge, which was situated in Brooklyn, this bar was owned by Roy. After this initial introduction Peter began to learn that Roy was heavily involved in auto-theft and was exporting stolen cars to order.

After a short while Calabro began to do little jobs here and there for Roy, giving him tip offs on raids or information on those who were snitching on Roy. Calabro would pocket good sums of money from doing this and eventually became involved in more schemes with Roy.

Peter and Roy began to collaborate in the exportation of stolen cars. This began after Roy had learned that Calabro was able to bypass VIN checks on vehicles. Peter made a deal with Roy whereby he would collect $1500 each week from Roy in exchange for checking the VIN numbers on the stolen cars before they were due to be exported.

As Peter Calabro's scheming ways grew at work his home life wasn't much better. In 1973 Peter had married an Italian American woman called Carmella Gentile. At first things had seemed fine between them, they were living together and seemed like your typical couple. That changed however, they hadn't been married too long when they separated in 1976, Carmella left Peter.

It was the 19th of June on a warm afternoon in 1977 almost a year after Carmella had left Peter. Peter and Carmella had decided to take a walk together and talk. They met up on Coney Island beach in Long Branch, New Jersey that afternoon. Carmella wasn't seen alive again after that. Her body was found floating in a river 5 days later on the 28th of July 1977 by local coast guards.

Due to Peter being a police officer himself the investigation into her murder was handed to NYPD Chief John Guido who was assisted by Captain Jimmy Skennion. After a bit of digging Guido discovered from witnesses that Peter and Carmella were seen walking together a very short time before she went missing. As a result of this and other suspicions Peter was arrested in 1977 for her suspected murder. Guido had sought an indictment against Calabro for Carmella's murder, but the courts didn't grant it after deciding there wasn't sufficient evidence.

It was rumoured that after the case fell through and no charges were made against Calabro for her murder, Carmella's brothers had taken matters into their own hands. They were convinced that Peter Calabro was the one responsible for their sisters' death. Guido said that he believed under good authority that the brothers had since hired someone to arrange Peter Calabro's murder. Detective Guido had reason to believe that the person the Gentile Brothers had hired was a man by the name of Salvatore Gravano.

Salvatore was not a man to be messed about with, he took the business of murder very seriously. On the street he was known to many as Sammy The Bull an underboss of the Gambino Crime family. With a ruthless reputation for violence and murder. Sammy knew plenty of unsavoury characters, for him it wouldn't be difficult to get the job done.

Sammy was later convicted of 19 mafia associated murders during a trial in September of 1992, after he confessed and took a plea deal. He is suspected of committing many more murders that he will never be convicted for.

After Guido hadn't got the indictment he wanted, he had to let the link to Calabro rest, they couldn't obtain anymore evidence against him and had come to a dead end.

Meanwhile Calabro had continued with his life at the NYPD after everything had died down. Carmellas family hadn't let the issue they had with Calabro go, the two Gentile brothers had made threats to Calabro on a few occasions. They were still convinced he was the one responsible for Carmellas death.

They had been watching him and found out he was doing deals with auto theft rings and were seen on one occasion outside the Gemini lounge watching Calabro.
Peter was still working jobs with Roy DeMeo and giving out information for cash, he would visit the lounge in Brooklyn to pass on messages to Roy.

It didn't take long for Peter to move on from Carmella, he had begun dating again. He ended up remarrying a woman he met shortly after Carmella's death called Stephanie, and they moved to a home in Upper Saddle River in New Jersey.

There were moments when Calabro would learn information about informants the police had. If these informants jeopardised anything he was involved with, he would sabotage police efforts by warning criminals that they were being informed on. One of these criminals was Roy DeMeo. When Calabro had learned of a letter being written to the police by another associate named Khaled Daoud, with a confession to crimes involving Roy, he immediately went to Roy to tell him.

After Roy left their meeting he was with his associate Dominik Montiglio and made a comment to Dominick that Calabro was indirectly responsible for some of the contracted hits Roy had arranged, and that Calabros information had caused many to meet their end. This wasn't the first time Dominick had heard DeMeo talk about Calabro. Roy had mentioned being irritated that he had to pay Calabro $1500 per week to pass the VIN number checks on the stolen cars at times before this. He thought it was an expense he could do without, but begrudgingly knew he had no choice if he wanted those cars to leave the pier.

It was early 1980 and life had almost gone back to normal for Peter Calabro. After a long shift at work he was on his way home. It was the early hours of March 14th, 1980, it had been snowing badly over the last few days and the roads were covered in snow, this night was no different. As the snow cascaded down at a blinding rate it had become hard to drive safely. Drivers had no choice but to take their time driving through the snowstorm. As Peter approached the road that led to his home he started to slow to make the turn off.

It was about 2am as Calabro started his slow drive down to Upper Saddle River, the road was long and surrounded by giant trees either side of it. In the snow it looked picturesque but dangerous nonetheless.

As Peter looked on ahead he saw what looked like a van partially blocking the road. He knew he would have to slow down to drive around it, checking for oncoming traffic at the same time. As he slowed, he could just make out his way around the van, he edged towards it, driving forwards. As he did this and got the front of his car passed the front door of the van, there was a sudden movement at the front of the van.

Startled Calabro pressed down his breaks and looked dead ahead squinting to try and see, as he did this there was a loud bang and a flash of light.

Peter Calabros body was found that same morning still in his car. He died from 2 fatal shotgun wounds to his head. After the crime scene was processed the investigation began into his death.

When questioned Calabros current wife Stephanie said she believed it was connected with Carmellas family. Stephanie reported that she had heard Carmellas parents James and Louise Gentile threaten Peter. She told the investigator that a few weeks before Peter was shot she saw Carmella's two brothers sitting outside her house watching it. The police tried to obtain a warrant to gain access to the Gentiles property but the courts denied them one. After hitting dead ends the case became cold.

It was 1981 and the auto theft crime unit had also become interested in Calabros connections with certain people. Upon further investigation into separate cases of mafia surveillance operations Peter Calabro's involvement in organised crime had begun to surface. Roughly 3 years later the investigation had revealed Calabro's connection with organised crime.

By 1984, the now deceased Calabro and 4 other former members of the auto crime division were all under investigation. Including Calabro's friend and work partner John Doherty. With allegations of selling sensitive information on auto theft investigations to the Gambino crime family in New York and New Jersey.

An associate of Roy DeMeo, a Mr Fredrick DiNome testified as a witness to some of the crimes Calabro and other officers carried out. DiNome was asked in what capacity was Calabro and John Doherty's involvement and if they received money from checking the VIN numbers on cars. They were asked "Did Calabro and Doherty receive money?" He replied "Yes, sometimes $2,000 or $3,000 a week, depending on how many cars were involved," - Mr. DiNome (1986). Peters death was still unsolved. There was someone who knew what happened to him, they just hadn't said anything yet.

It was 2001 and Richard Kuklinski was getting ready to film the last of a series of interviews for television. He had been incarcerated for about 15 years now for the murders he committed. This interview was going to pique the interest of law enforcement all over again.

Richard describes a murder he had committed for Salvatore Gravano in exchange for money. He very calmly elaborates carrying out the murder. He explains it was 1980 around March, he had been contacted about doing a hit for Sammy The Bull. After accepting the job he arranges to go and pick up the shotgun from Sammy. They discuss the plan and clarify the job. Richard had no interest in who the target was or why they were a target, as long as the price was right

According to Richard it was late in the evening of March 13[th,] and he was getting ready to carry out the hit for Sammy. He was driving a van to the location to use as a block to slow traffic down. His job was helped by the fact it had been snowing heavily, meaning cars were having to drive more carefully anyway. He got into the van and slowly crept to Saddle River.

Once he arrived at the location he got out his walky-talky and started to look at the best spot in the road to stop at. He noticed that the road thinned out in one part so decided to stop the van there and pull out onto the road at a slight angle. Now cars would have to slow down to drive around him.

By this point it was the early hours of March 14th, Richard was in position, and he waited. Shortly before 2am he hears his walkie-talkie make a noise. It was a signal code to get into position. By this time there were little to no cars on the road, it was snowing and hard to see anything, so the cars were coming down the road at a snail pace. Richard knew once he heard the next signal, the next car to roll by would be his target.

He crouches down by the front of his van just out of sight of the oncoming cars. He glances behind him to check there are no cars coming from the others side, and gets ready to make his move. It hard to see with the snow against his face but he can here the soft noise of an engine. As it gets closer he steps out into the road and shoots towards the head of the silhouette he can see in the car windshield.

He glances into the car to make sure the man is dead and gets back into the van, starts the engine and drives away. The next morning when Richard gets up the mans death is all over the news. He hears "Detective Peter Calabro shot to death in snowstorm". That was when he found out the man he shot was a police officer. Richard said he would have killed Calabro even if he had known he was a police officer.

This new information meant new investigation, the police had found links in Peters belongings that suggested he was affiliated with members of the Gambino's. Roy DeMeos personal home phone number was also recovered from Peters phone book. He had handwritten the number entry and it was stored under the name Roy. Now that these other links had begun to pop up it was time for the police to act.

With this confession came repercussions for Richard, in 2003 Richard was convicted for the murder of Peter Calabro. An extra 30 years was added to his current sentences for murder. Richard agreed to testify in court against Sammy the Bull who by this time was serving a 20 year sentence for 19 murders. Sammy was charged with conspiracy to murder and was due to appear in court for a trial.

Sammy and his lawyers adamantly denied these charges and Richards account of events. Sammy said he had nothing to do with Peter Calabro's death. Despite Richard being charged for the murder of Calabro it is disputed by some if Richard is the guilty one. Some of those who were involved closely with the case during the 1970's believe that it was Carmella's two brothers and not Richard. Sammy's lawyers also agree with these claims.

This doubt is not helped by Kuklinski's own actions either. During a meeting with Sammy's Lawyers Richard attempted to extort $200.000 from Sammy Gravano, in exchange for him to not testify against him. The claim of extortion was confirmed by the FBI who had evidence of a note that was written by Kuklinski to Sammy's lawyers stating he wanted to be paid for his silence.

There are some however, who say they can support Richards allegations that Sammy was responsible for the organisation of Calabros murder. A number of other witnesses and informants had also come forward stating that they had heard Sammy talking about the murder, some even said he had bragged about it.

The Mafia in general have a rule that they don't kill cops, it draws too much attention and can interfere with business for them. This is not a new rule it has been one of the core rules since their establishment. It wouldn't be strange if Sammy had involvement in Calabro's death. But with that said it also wouldn't be that strange for them to hire a person who wasn't associated to them, to carry out a hit on a cop.

Someone they knew had the ability to do the job, take the money, no questions asked. Kuklinski fits this profile, he had no real known links to them, which meant that detectives would be looking at Kuklinski and not at the Gambino's if there ever was an investigation.

The Gambino members would have no reason to admit to any of this to verify what Kuklinski had said, they gain nothing from that. What happens to Richard is of no concern to them, they know his links to them are minimal. This was also the way Richard operated he would maintain a distance with most of his business associates specifically so he couldn't be linked to them.

Sammy had taken a plea deal; part of this deal was that he disclosed the information of all the murders he had committed previously in exchange for a reduced sentence. He claimed that he had confessed all murders he was responsible for. If he was the one who had organised Peter Calabro's murder then he would have breached the terms of the plea deal. This could have dire consequences for Sammy. It was in his best interests to deny any involvement with this case whatsoever.

Ultimately Richard was the one charged with Peter Calabro's death, he knew details about the case that only certain people would know so it is very possible given Richards past that he committed this murder for money. Even with Richard's confession there are possibilities that he didn't carry out this murder and it was like others have said. It was actually a revenge kill of a grief stricken family.

9

Louis L Masgay

July 1st, 1981

Louis L Masgay was born April 11th, 1931. At the time of his death July 1st, 1981, he was living in Forty Fort in Luzerne County, Pennsylvania, with his wife and children. Louis was the owner of a discount store in Plymouth, Pennsylvania, called Leisure City and was well known by his local customers.

He lived a life of habit and was a predictable man according to his wife. She said he liked routine, and never really behaved out of the ordinary. He had a time he liked to be home by, a time when he liked to sit down and eat as a family. A regular day to day flow, that would rarely alter. As a family they lived a simple yet content life.

The store was becoming a true family business once his son Lou Jr began working with his father. They would share jobs and Lou Jr would often help with the collection and drop off of stock. Accompanying his father to business meetings with suppliers and stockists.

The Masgay family were by no means well off financially but progressing well with the business. It was attracting regular custom and Masgay was confident it would keep getting better as long as he offered stock at low prices. He would put in the work looking for suppliers who had deals that meant the profit margin was too good to turn down.

Louis Masgay was not a known associate of Kuklinski's, he was introduced to Richard via the purchase and sale of stolen goods. On one of his many hunts for stock he was pointed in the direction of Richard.

Upon meeting Kuklinski he was offered one of these deals, one he just couldn't refuse. Masgay knew Richard Kuklinski dealt with film and video tape distribution, so when Richard said he could get his hands on large quantities of blank video tapes it didn't seem strange. Richard was in this business after all, it would make sense that he would bump into film and tape suppliers from time to time.

Masgay knew the tapes would sell well in his store, it was a sure-fire bet, he'd be a fool to turn down such a good deal. With that in mind Masgay organised an exchange with Richard, they settled a price and day to meet. Talking on the phone to decide a time and place to meet before they went ahead with the exchange.

The first few times they were due to meet Masgay would drive to New Jersey with the cash. Once he arrived, he would contact Richard from a payphone, only to be told by Richard the deal was off. Richard would say his guy (the supplier) had got cold feet and backed out at the last minute. Or that Richards supplier didn't believe Masgay had the cash so would refuse to come.

This happened several times, five in total. Each time there would be a problem, Richard would assure Masgay he would find another guy. Each time Richard found another guy the price would go up.

This didn't put Masgay off the purchase, even with the increases in price the deal itself was still very cheap for the amount of stock Masgay would be receiving.

By the fifth time of cancelling Masgay decided to give the deal one last go, if it fell through again, he was going to tell Richard the deal was off. He wasn't interested in the video tapes anymore.

July 1st 1981, Louis Masgay gets his van ready for the trip to Little Ferry New Jersey. He brings $95,000 in cash, which he hides in a concealed compartment in the driver door of his van. Getting this cash together had not been easy for Masgay, he had used all his savings plus a bank loan of $45,000 to make up the amount Richard had asked for. Saying goodbye to his wife, he let her know he would be back later that evening and that he shouldn't be gone for long.

He headed to New Jersey shortly after this, on arrival he had planned to meet his son Lou at the Golden star diner for a coffee. Lou was travelling through; it was a spot they would often meet up in. As they sat drinking their coffee discussing the video tape deal, Lou asked his father if he wanted help loading up the van, he knew it was a big order and thought it would save his father some time and effort.

Masgay respectfully declined and told Lou not to worry, he would be fine. He told him to make his way home and that he would be back himself in a few hours. After Lou left the diner Masgay contacted Richard. This time Richard said everything was going as planned, his guy was coming with the tapes and that Masgay should make his way to the meeting point.

Arriving at the location Masagy parked up and got out of his van, making his way over to Kuklinski. There was a bit of small talk, Richard said his guy was on route with the tapes and wouldn't be long.

Richard couldn't see where Masgays money was, so asked him if he definitely had the full amount. He told Masgay he didn't want to look the fool if the guy showed up and there wasn't enough cash. Masgay insisted to Richard he had the cash and as soon as the guy showed up, he would get it out and ready.

They were waiting a while and by this point no one had come, Masgay getting anxious asked Richard if he was sure the guy was coming? Hoping he hadn't pulled out of the deal last minute like the times before. Masgay was getting fed up of the wasted trips by this point so his patience was running thin.

Richard reassured him the guy was on the way and that he would be here any minute now. Again, Richard brings up the money asking Louis Masgay if he has the full $95,000 he would need to get it out ready. Masgay heads towards the driver side of the van and opened the door. He ushered Richard to come and look inside. As Richard got closer behind him, he peered over Masgays shoulder into the door of the van where he saw Masgay open a hidden compartment.

"See Rich" said Masgay, "I told you it's all here don't worry." Before Masgay could take another breath to speak Richard shot him in the back of the head. He slumped down folding into himself.

Richard then leaned over and took the $95.000 that was hidden in the door of Masgay's van and put it with his things. He then calmly picked up Masgays now dead body moving him away from the van and laid him out on the floor. Kuklinski proceeded to meticulously wrap Louis Masgay in layer after layer of garbage bags until his whole body had been concealed. This took a while, there were 15-20 layers of bags according to police records.

Once Masgays body was wrapped up Richard hid his body in a large freezer in a garage for almost two years. Richards reasoning for this was to distort time of death making it much harder for the police to link the death of Louis to him.

He then took the van and drove it to an unconnected location to dump it. Before leaving he made sure the tank was empty and anything that might connect him to the crime had been removed. Pleased with himself Kuklinski then made his way home to tell his wife Barbara they had come into a bit of money from one of his business deals.

Back in Pennsylvania Louis Masgays wife was becoming anxious, she had not heard from Louis for hours now, which was very unusual. Even if Louis was just running behind on time he would always contact her to let her know, he knew otherwise she would worry about him.

By midnight she still hadn't heard anything from Louis, she picked up the phone and called the police to report him as missing. The report was logged with detective Henry Winters, who made notes on everything Mrs Masgay said. He told her he would make it his priority to look into this and that he would get in touch with New Jersey Law Enforcement to file a missing report in their jurisdiction too.

A few days after Detective Winters had contacted the New Jersey Police force, he was notified that Louis Masgays van had been found abandoned on a narrow part of the road just off route 17 North by Rochelle Park in Bergen, NJ. In the report it noted that the doors to the van were locked and the police had broken a window to gain access to the vehicle. They also noted that only one of the fuel tanks had been emptied but the second was still full.

Despite Henry Winters best efforts to pursue the missing Louis Masgay, it was out of his jurisdiction and there was only so much he could do. He had shared his statements and information with New Jersey state police. These statements included the information that Masgay was meeting a man to do a business deal on goods for resale. It included this mans name, yet it seemed the officers handling the case didn't look into this any further, nor did it seem like it was their priority.

Almost two years later Masgays body would be found.

Eventually Richard decided it was time to discard of Louis Masgay. He had been keeping the body in a freezer the whole time, just waiting for the right time and place to dump it. He decided it had been long enough, the investigation on Masgay had died down by this point, he had heard nothing from the police so figured they weren't actively looking for him.

Richard dumped Masgays body on a warm September evening, defrosting, but not defrosted. Richard knew it wouldn't take too long for the body to warm up. Then it would look like a recent thing Richard thought, not something that had happened years ago. He decided not to do it in New Jersey, after all he had gone to all this trouble, he wasn't going to leave it anywhere local to himself, that wouldn't be wise.
Afterwards still feeling confident about his plan to deceive Law Enforcement he drove home.

As Masgays body defrosted, it was found by a park ranger on September 25, 1983, near a park off Clausland Mountain Road, Orangetown, New York.

Speaking to Masgays wife they found out that the day of his disappearance he was due to meet a man by the name of Richard Kuklinski. That he had left his hometown late in the afternoon on July 1st, 1981. They also saw the report noted the description of the clothes Louis had been wearing the day he disappeared. One of the investigators thought it was very strange that the clothes Louis Masgay had been found in were the same clothes he had vanished in 15 months ago.

Initially the police had no idea that the body had been frozen, this was not identified until the autopsy was carried out. Once they knew it had been frozen, they realised that it had not happened recently and started to investigate Masgays whereabouts the day he was reported missing by his family. The investigation into Kuklinski had begun.

It was this information and the act of freezing the body that earned Richard Kuklinski the now infamous nickname 'The Iceman' which was given to him by the police force investigating the Masgay Murder.

10

Paul Hoffman

April 29th, 1982

Last seen alive April 1982. The Pharmacist was tricked into thinking he was buying prescription drugs (Tagamet) from Richard, that he could then sell on at a higher price. There never were any drugs. It was a con.

He had met Richard in a store in Paterson, a place many criminals and con men visited to purchase contraband and stolen goods from. At the time, Paul was looking for cheap drugs he could sell under the counter in his pharmacy.

He initially had spoken to another person about getting the drugs he needed, but they had grown tired of Pauls consistent pestering about getting him the Tagamet. Hoping Paul would leave him alone he had told Paul to ask Richard Kuklinski about getting them figuring that Paul would see Richard and knowing his reputation be too intimidated to approach him.

Instead, Paul went right up to Richard and said that he had heard Richard was the guy to come to for things. Rather than ask for the Tagamet outright and get a bad reaction from Richard, Paul decided to ask him about buying some samples of the porn he made. In Pauls mind he could establish a connection this way and soften Richard up a bit before he asked him about getting the drugs, he wanted. After buying some tapes from Richard he felt as though he could now ask him about other things. Things like prescription drugs.

Richard of course saw the man's desperation, it oozed out of him, and to Richard desperation means extortion. Seeing this as a good opportunity to make some money Kuklinski told Paul he could get what he wanted, he had a guy.

Over some weeks they exchanged in conversation, Richard would set up the deal and then cancel on Paul. His plan was to put Paul off the sale by pretending his guy got cold feet and backed out. Then he could up the price and tell Paul he found a new guy but it would cost a bit more. Each time upping the price. This was a technique Richard had used successfully before.

Paul became extremely desperate and insisted that Richards guy do the exchange. He told Richard he had the money there ready, he needed to get the Tagamet now or he would go out of business and then there really would be no more deal.

Richard agreed to a meeting to do the exchange. Paul arrived unaware it was all a set up, they both sat waiting for Richards "guy" to arrive. He was getting impatient and asked Richard where the merchandise was. Insisting he has the money he just wants the deal done.

Paul made his way to the back of his truck and ushered Richard towards the spare tire compartment in the trunk of the truck. Richards eyes widened as he saw the cash, it was all there just like Paul had said.

As he leaned forward to look at the cash Richard proceeded to pull out his gun and place it under Paul's chin. "There is no merchandise" Richard said as he pulled the trigger. The gun shot out and Paul fell to the floor gagging, grasping at his throat injured but not dead. Richard went to shoot again but, the gun jammed which left Paul Hoffman alive but barely.

Not wanting to leave him alive, Richard looked around for something to finish the job, he saw a tire iron which was already at the location. He reached over and grabbed it, proceeding to beat Hoffman over the head with it until he had died.

Richard then took the cash Hoffman had bought with him for the exchange which totalled to $22.000, he wiped down the tire iron and put it back where he had found it. Then began to dispose of Hoffman's body.

Richard put Hoffman's body into a metal drum and sealed it in concrete. For roughly a month he stored it in the garage then he decided to move it. Richard left the barrel outside Harrys Corner Luncheonette on the Boardwalk, Wildwood. NJ.

The drum went missing after a while, Richard didn't know what happened to it. He would visit the cafe daily to see if it was still there, then one day it was just gone. Paul Hoffman's body has never been recovered.

11

Gary Smith

December 23rd, 1982

Gary Smith was an associate of Richards, he was one of four members of Richards burglary gang. He worked under the instruction of Richard and a man named Percy House. They had been working together for a couple of years and would carry out car thefts and burglaries almost on a weekly basis. Gary specialised in car theft and was very efficient at it too. He would work alongside a man named Daniel Deppner who was just as good as stealing as Gary was.

Gary and Daniel were friends through Daniels ex-wife Barbara, who was also Gary's cousin. The two men spent a lot of time together. In general both had similar interests and similar criminal abilities. But they were nothing alike personality wise. Gary thought Daniel was a bit of a push over, at times and didn't have a whole lot of respect for him because of this.

He would watch as Percy would bully Daniel, he would beat on Daniel often knowing that Daniel wouldn't fight back. Daniel was scared of him and did whatever Percy asked. Percy took full advantage of this. Despite being married Percy had taken a liking to Daniels wife Barbara and they had begun to have an affair together. Both Gary and Daniel were aware of this relationship and Daniel just accepted it and did nothing, eventually leaving his wife Barbara.

Gary was a family man, he was married with a daughter, over the years as he watched his daughter grow up he started to realise this wasn't the life he wanted anymore. He wanted to get out and go straight and be a better example for his child. This was harder than it sounded, first of all he would need to officially leave the theft gang. Trying to tell two huge violent paranoid men that he wanted out was an intimidating thought.

He knew how Percy would react and expected him to have an outburst about it. This didn't fuss Gary so much he could deal with Percy, it was Richards reaction that he feared the most. He knew Richard wouldn't want to hear what he was saying and probably wouldn't accept it either. Regardless of his worries he told the rest of the gang he wanted out. That he didn't want to make a fuss about it, he just wanted to leave quietly and get a legitimate job.

Both Percy and Richard dismissed Gary's request, he was told he couldn't leave because he would rat them out to the police. Gary insisted he didn't want to tell the police anything he just wanted to leave. That they didn't need to worry about him snitching on them because he had no intentions to do that. He was told clearly there was no getting out, that he would continue to work for them and not to complain about it.

It had been a couple of months since Gary had announced that he wanted to leave the gang. Nothing had changed he was still doing jobs for Percy and Richard, only now they seemed to be in a constant bad mood with him. He knew in the back of his mind it was because they saw him as a liability, so he just kept quiet about it all.

After Lieutenant Pat Kane had spent the last year building a case against them he was ready to seek indictments for each of them and presented his case in court. After hearing the evidence Pat Kane had obtained, the court had issued warrants for the men's arrests. Between the 4 men they had a total of 153 charges that had been bought against them.

It was December 17th, Gary, Daniel, Barbara and Percy were in Barbara's car with the kids on their way to her mother's house. When they noticed police cars parked up at the end of her mother's street. Feeling uneasy at the sight of them, Percy told Daniel and Gary to get out of the car and hide, so they weren't all seen together. They stopped the car before turning into the street and let Gary and Daniel out.

Barbara turned onto the road and made her way to her mothers house as she went to turn into the drive, police cars had blocked her in. There was a rush of confusion as the police stormed the car, pulling out Percy House in the process. Percy was yelling and cursing by this point the kids and Barbara were frantic.

Once Percy was arrested he was held for questioning. Barbara had taken the children into her mothers house to calm them down and made a call to Richard telling him what had happened. Richard was not happy at all, this was the last thing he needed. He told Barbara to find where Gary and Daniel were and to take them somewhere safe until he could speak to them.

A few hours after speaking to Richard she managed to see Gary and Daniel who by this point were extremely stressed out. They had no idea what was going on, all they knew was that they needed to lay low. Gary's wife had been in hysterics over the whole thing, they found out from her that the police had shown up at her house with warrants for both Gary and Daniel and a warrant to search their home. After questioning Gary's wife and getting no information from her about their whereabouts they had left.

She took Gary and Daniel to a motel just outside of their local area. telling them both to wait there and stay inside the room until she could find out what was going on. She hadn't got a call from Percy yet and was getting concerned, she didn't have much money and couldn't afford to keep renting out motel rooms for them. Knowing Richard wanted to be kept informed she had contacted him to tell him the situation.

Upon hearing that Barbara couldn't keep putting the men up in motels he arranged to meet them at a diner to take over. Barbara took them to Richard where he told them that he would be putting them up in motels and that there were rules. They could not leave the room or make calls unless Richard had agreed to it. They were not to talk to people or give anyone their real names.

They arrived at a motel called The Liberty, this would be their home for the next few days at least. Richard orders Daniel to go and book the room under the name Jack Bush, then tells him to come straight back to the car. Once the men had settled into their room Barbara left, leaving them with Richard.

After their meeting Barbara headed back to her sisters to get the kids, it had been two days and she hadn't heard from Percy. This was playing on her mind, she needed to speak to him to find out what the situation was. The police agreed to let her visit Percy, by this point 3 days had gone by. Percy wasn't pleased when he saw Barbara, she could see it in his eyes despite his smile. He greeted her and acted happy knowing the prison guards were watching them and listening in.

They started to chat, Barbara hinted that the two men were safe and sound but Percy had another thing on his mind. Percy got straight to the point. He told Barbara that he had a message for Richard. The message was simple "send Gary to Florida" as he said this he grinned at her barely moving his lips to sound out the sentence. Barbara's heart sunk into her feet; she could feel all the colour in her face drain away. She nods back to Percy in agreement, and they continue their visit, before she makes her way home.

Later that day Barbara made her way to the motel to see Richard and give him the message from Percy. When she told Richard what Percy had said, Richard didn't react, she went to repeat herself but he interrupted her letting her know he understood.

Barbara noticed that Gary had a black eye, she couldn't help but stare at it, Daniel saw her fixated gaze and said to her that Gary hadn't obeyed the rules. Turning her head to look straight at Richard she knew what had happened and that the black eye was courtesy of him. She found out that Gary had snuck out of the motel, he had stolen from a local gas station and then hitchhiked to go and see his daughter.

After hearing Barbaras message from Percy and then finding out about Garys little misadventure, Richard was growing tired of him. Gary had become a huge liability, he wasn't to be trusted. He couldn't go even a single day without putting himself in a situation where he could be caught. Richard knew if the police were called over his theft at the gas station that would be it. Gary would squeal.

Percy was right thought Richard, Gary did need to go to Florida.

For Richard the cons started to outweigh the pros when it came to keeping Gary around. In fact, the whole ordeal had become costly for Richard in multiple ways. He was footing the bill for the rooms, food, and other necessities.

This would have to continue for as long as Law Enforcement were looking for them, Richard knew they would keep pursuing them. He knew that if Gary was alive, he was a potential liability.

It was December 23rd and the men had been on the run for 6 days. It hadn't taken long for Richard to grow tired of the trips to the motel, by now they were at the York Motel in bergen NJ. The added expenses and time all of this was taking got Richards mind working overtime, just one mistake and that could be it, Richard would get arrested. He couldn't have that, he had put time and effort into not getting caught. All those years of illegitimate behaviour undetected by authorities. It needed to stay that way he thought to himself.

As Richard would regularly bring them both food, he decided the best way to kill Gary, was using cyanide. He told Daniel that he was going to "send Gary to Florida" and that he was to help Richard get rid of the body afterwards. Daniel was instructed to speak to Barbara and tell her to make sure the car was ready for them at the motel that night.

Richard left his home cyanide in hand and made his way to get the food. Richard ordered 3 burger meals, two burgers with pickles and one burger without. This would be an easy way to identify which burger was for Gary. Before making his way to the motel room he took the pickle-less burger out of its wrapper, lifting off the top of the burger bun he added the cyanide. As he finished wrapping the burger back up, he focused his thoughts, and made his way to the door.

Inside the room everything seemed normal, the atmosphere was calm, and nothing looked out of place.

Richard placed the burgers down on the side and started to take them out, paying extra attention to make sure each person got the right meal.

As Gary ate the laced burger, he seemed to have little to no reaction to the cyanide. Both Richard and Daniel stared intently as he ate it, on edge, knowing what should be happening but wasn't.

Then it happened, he began to gasp and gargle, thrashing about grabbing at his face and throat. Richard started to laugh as he saw Gary struggle, but this chuckle faded out. Why wasn't Gary dead yet? Richard thought, somethings not right he should be dead by now. Becoming impatient and annoyed at the fuss Gary was making, Richard ordered Daniel to strangle him.

Daniel looking around the room for something he could use he saw the lamp. Gary still thrashing about and making strange noises wasn't letting up. Using the cord of the lamp Daniel approached Gary from the side of the bed reaching the cord around and pulling it tight and twisting, strangling Gary. As he tightened the cord, he could hear Richard laughing, telling him to hurry up and get it done, people might have heard all the commotion.

Gary's body took a while to go limp, what seemed like an eternity to Daniel, he slowly released his grip moving the cord away from Garys neck. Gary just lay there lifeless on the bed next to his pickle-less burger. While Daniel stares at him blankly, Richard had already moved on to the next issue, getting rid of Gary's body.

Richard had initially planned to move Gary's body by car then find somewhere to store it, but this plan backfired when Barbara Deppner hadn't returned with the car that was meant to be used. Not happy about this Richard decided to improvise. He made his way to the bed and told Daniel they were going to put Gary inside the box frame and that they needed to leave as soon as possible. They then stuffed Gary's body between the mattress and the bed frame and left it there.

On December 27, 1982, 4 days after they had killed him Gary Smiths body was discovered by people staying in the room, who had noticed a foul smell coming from the bed.

12

Daniel Deppner

February 1983

Daniel Deppner met Kuklinski through the criminal work they did. He was also a thief who specialised in stealing cars, he worked alongside Gary Smith. For a while, he was married to Gary's cousin Barbara.

Over time Daniel became an associate of Richards, he would do jobs under Richards instruction. Eventually he would end up working for Kuklinski, under Percy House in the breaking and entering gang.

Daniel Deppner was a married man but was no longer with his wife. His wife Barbara Deppner was well aware of his criminal life. She wasn't a stranger to the group and at times would help out with jobs and menial tasks that the gang had. Often, she would be taking calls and passing on messages or doing pick-ups and drop offs. She knew each of the four men but wasn't so well known to Kuklinski.

Barbara would eventually leave Daniel for one of the ringleaders Percy House. She would end up living with Percy and Daniel moved out of the marital bedroom. Daniel and Barbara remained married but were by all accounts separated. Barbara still did things for the burglary group even after she left Daniel. Being in a relationship with Percy meant she was still involved with some things, so would be in contact with them on a regular basis.

After years of committing burglaries and being involved with money making scams, the police had their eye on the group of men. Deppner had been indicted in Passaic County "on more than 70 counts of operating in a North Jersey burglary ring that specialised in stolen cars" NJ Herald (1986) Both Deppner and Smith had also been indicted in a bad check scheme in Sussex county in April of 1983.

With the law closing in on them it all started to fall apart, their houses had been searched. Their families had been questioned, after Percy House had been arrested it began to crumble. Percy House had been one of those giving orders, just like Richard he didn't exactly have a reputation of being a nice person. A plan had been devised between Richard and Percy to kill Gary Smith. Both Richard and Percy felt that Gary was a liability and needed to be killed.

Daniel helped Richard with the death of Gary Smith, he told his ex-wife Barbara what he had done. When he spoke to her, he told her what happened, that the poison wasn't enough to kill him. He said how Richard had laughed at Gary when he was being poisoned. He told her Richard said to finish him off, so he had taken a lamp and used the cord to choke Gary until he went limp and died.

He explained to her that Gary looked funny after he died, and his eyes were all "googley". He went on to explain how they had put Gary's body under the motel bed in between the box frame under the mattress. And that they had just left the motel to find somewhere else to stay. He told her Richard had said someone else could clean him up.

Barbara didn't want to hear anymore; she asked Daniel to stop. Gary was her cousin she already wasn't coping well just knowing he was going to be killed. The last thing she wanted to hear about was all the grizzly details of it happening. The less she knew about this whole thing the better, she had almost become a nervous wreck.

Richard had decided motels by this point were a no go. Instead, he put Daniel into an apartment, this wasn't a property that was in Richards name. It was an apartment registered to the name of a man called Rich Patterson. Rich Patterson was the fiancé of Richard Kuklinski's daughter.

Once Daniel was in the apartment Richards paranoia continued to grow. He had a nagging thought in the back of his head that Daniel would get scared and go to the police. He couldn't trust Daniel, at all, even if he kept him under surveillance what next? He would remain a problem as long as he was alive, he was a liability.

The only way Richard could see of getting rid of this problem, was to get rid of Daniel too. If he did this right, it would just seem like the two had fled and gone on the run after hearing they were wanted in the string of burglaries. Then all the loose ends would be tied up. He began to devise a plan to kill Daniel Deppner.

The exact date of Daniels death is not known but it is assumed he was killed around February in 1983.

He was killed in the apartment he was staying in courtesy of Kuklinski. Just like Gary he was poisoned and then strangled. Evidence at the crime scene included two plastic food tubs found on the kitchen counter. The same food tubs Richard Kuklinski had in his home.

After killing Daniel Richard went about disposing of his body and covering the crime. Richard wrapped Daniels body in layers of plastic bags ready to be removed. He cleaned the carpet in the room because some of Daniels blood had got onto it. Then took Daniels body away to be stored until he could dump it somewhere.

Eventually Richard enlisted Rich Pattersons help in disposing of Daniels body. Rich had driven with Kuklinski to get rid of what he claimed he thought was rubbish. He said he was unaware he had helped to transport a dead body.

Daniels body was dumped along the Clinton Road in West Milford, New Jersey. It laid there decomposing until it was found on May 14th, 1983, by a passing cyclist.

13

Robert Prongay
aka
Mister Softee

August 8th, 1984

There has been a lot of speculation around if Mister Softee was even a real person. It has been claimed by many that he was just a figment of Kuklinski's imagination, just another lie Richard had told to inflate his own ego.

However, this is not true. Mister Softee was indeed a real person. He rented garage space where he kept his ice cream truck, this was next to a property Richard Kuklinski rented on Newkirk Ave & 70th St, North Bergen, NJ 07047.

Richard had claimed to know this man through a coincidence. Both he and Robert were essentially staking out the same person. They were both watching someone who was marked for a hit. This is apparently how they became acquainted.

Richard described Robert as a military trained hitman who used the disguise of an ice cream vendor to stake out his victims for hired hits.

He said Robert had extensive knowledge of chemicals, weapons, explosives, and body disposal. Richard explained he had learned some of his techniques such as the spray bottles of liquid cyanide and freezing bodies to distort time of death, from Robert.

During Richards interviews he speaks about storing a victim's body in a freezer which was kept in Roberts garage. It is suspected that this was the body of Louis Masgay. Most of Richard's claims about Robert regarding his distaste for his family, by all accounts can be verified by police records. He had a criminal history for harassing and attempting to harm his family. He did want his wife and son dead and was actively trying to kill them.

Robert Joseph Prongay was born December 30, 1945, in New Jersey. To his Father Robert Prongay and Mother Sarah Prongay (maiden name Healy). Robert was a twin to his brother Kevin.

As a teen he attended Union Hill High School in New Jersey, (closed in 2008), and can be found in an image from the 1963 yearbook on page 47 alongside his twin brother Kevin Prongay.

He was an ice cream man who did indeed have a criminal record for things such as explosives, among other crimes. He was married and fathered two children, as well as living and working in New Jersey.

Robert's behaviour towards his ex-wife Ellen and their child John was violent and threatening. He essentially terrorised them, attempting multiple times to injure and kill them.

During mid 1983 Robert had acquired a significant number of fireworks; he was planning to use these to create homemade bombs. These bombs would be used to blow up his ex-wife's home along with his ex-wife and son.

On the 9th of August 1983 he planted two of the homemade bombs inside the home of his estranged family. They both went off causing damage to the building, but luckily Ellen and John were okay. Ellen reported the incident to the police soon after.

Angry that his attempt at killing them had failed he returned on October 31st, 1983, in a car and waited for them. Upon seeing Ellen and John he proceeded to drive towards them yelling that he was going to kill them both, and he wanted them dead no matter what. Driving erratically at them nearly injuring his son in the process, John and Ellen dart out of the way and get to safety.

Once Ellen had access to a phone, she reported the incident to the police. The police went out to Robert's place of residence on the 7th of November 1983 to speak to him about the reports his ex-wife had made. He refused them entry and wouldn't speak to them.

On Tuesday, 8th of November they came back with a warrant and forced entry into the property. Once they gained entry they found and seized what was described as, "a cache of fireworks" – The Jersey Journal (1983)

Prongay was indicted on charges of – aggravated assault, arson, terroristic threats, and contempt of court.

He was due in court on Wednesday, 8th August 1984, for the bombing of his ex-wife's home. He also had convictions for trying to run over his son with a car. He had been granted bail which was set at $10,000, with instructions not to go near his ex-wife or son in the meantime.

When the day came for Robert to be in court he was nowhere to be seen. Attempts by the court to contact him had not been successful. When it became clear he wasn't intending to come to court Judge Joseph Thuring issued a bench warrant for his arrest and law enforcement began to look for him.

When the police learned of the garage, he was renting they decided to go and scope the area out. Upon arrival they found the garage door unlocked and ajar.
Detective Peter Ziembardo and Detective Leonard Cattaneo discovered Robert Prongays body.

When they entered the property Roberts body was found, "hanging out of the driver's side door of his ice cream truck with two bullet holes in his chest" The Jersey Journal (1984).

His body was discovered on Friday, 10th August 1984 and his death was reported by the papers on Saturday, 11th August 1984.

It is suspected that Robert died on Thursday 09th August 1984 aged 38.

So, who shot Robert? Was it Richard Kuklinski?

Richard has verbally taken responsibility for the death of Robert Prongay. Despite this no charges were brought against Richard, due to lack of evidence connecting him to the crime. So Prongays death remains unsolved.

Richard claimed that Robert Prongay had asked him to carry out a hit on his family, something that disgusted Richard. Robert had spoken about this with Richard a few times, essentially brainstorming his ideas to Richard about getting rid of his family.

Richard mentions that Prongay even suggested poisoning the local water source just to accomplish this.

The thought of a man willing to have his wife and child executed made Richard's blood boil. Richard claims he had shot Robert there and then. Upon realising Robert was completely serious about killing Ellen and John, he decided couldn't stand for that. So, he took care of the problem, then just walked off leaving Roberts body for someone else to clean up.

There is no evidence to support Richard's claims that Robert Prongay was a hitman. Nor is there any evidence that supports the idea that Richard was the one who killed him.

That said, Robert Prongay was murdered in his ice cream truck, and did die of bullet wounds. Police and news reports would also indicate that Robert seemed to be trying to kill his wife and child, at that time, like Richard had claimed. He did have some knowledge of explosives, and actively used that knowledge just like Richard had said.

The Bayonne Times   The Jersey Journal
Saturday, August 11, 1984
118th Year   No. 88

Article: "Man on trial shot to death"

By Jeff Pundyk and Frank Alkyer

"An ice-cream vendor who failed to appear at his trial for arson and aggravated assault was found shot to death yesterday in a North Bergen garage.

Robert Prongay, 39, of North Bergen was found hanging out of the driver's side door of his ice-cream truck with two bullet holes in his chest, according to police.

Prongay was on trial for the bombing of his ex-wife's house one year ago. He was also charged with aggravated assault and terroristic threats against his ex-wife and their teenage son.

The trial began Wednesday in front of Judge Joseph Thuring. On Thursday, Prongay who was out on $10,000 bail, didn't appear and a bench warrant was issued for his arrest.

Sheriff Dominick Pugliese said sheriff's detectives had searched for Prongay for a day and a half before learning Prongay parked his trucked in a garage at the corner of 70th and Newkirk streets.

Detectives Peter Ziembardo and Leonard Cattaneo, on investigating, found the garage door open. They found the body inside.

Early reports said Prongay's body had been found but did not mention the shooting.

Lt. Jerry Dargan of the Hudson County Homicide Strike Force later confirmed Prongay was shot to death.

No arrests have been made in connection with the incident. An autopsy is scheduled to be performed today.

According to court records Prongay was charged with causing an explosion at 3505 Charles Court, North Bergen. He also was charged with trying to run down Ellen Prongay, his ex-wife, and John Prongay, his son with a car and threatening to kill John.

His trial was being prosecuted by Assistant Prosecutor James Flynn."

THE BAYONNE TIMES

features now appearing in

THE JERSEY JOURNAL

Home Delivery $1.10 weekly

25 CENTS

Tonight: Mostly cloudy, low in 60s.
Tomorrow: Mostly cloudy, high in 80s.

SATURDAY, AUGUST 11, 1984

118th Year — No. 88

Man on trial shot to death

By Jeff Pundyk and Frank Alkyer

An ice-cream vendor who failed to appear at his trial for arson and aggravated assault was found shot to death yesterday in a North Bergen garage.

Robert Prongay, 39, of North Bergen was found hanging out of the driver's side door of his ice-cream truck with two bullet holes in his chest, according to police.

Prongay was on trial for the bombing of his ex-wife's house one year ago. He was also charged with aggravated assault and terroristic threats against his ex-wife and their teenage son.

The trial began Wednesday in front of Judge Joseph Thuring. On Thursday, Prongay, who was out on $10,000 bail, didn't appear and a bench warrant was issued for his arrest.

Sheriff Dominick Pugliese said sheriff's detectives had searched for Prongay for a day and a half before learning Prongay parked his truck in a garage at the corner of 70th and Newkirk streets.

Detectives Peter Ziembardo and Leonard Cattaneo, on investigating, found the garage door open. They found the body inside.

Early reports said Prongay's body had been found but did not mention the shooting.

Lt. Jerry Dargan of the Hudson County Homicide Strike Force later confirmed Prongay was shot to death.

No arrests have been made in connection with the incident. An autopsy is scheduled to be performed today.

According to court records, Prongay was charged with causing an explosion at 3566 Charles Court, North Bergen. He also was charged with trying to run down Ellen Prongay, his ex-wife, and John Prongay, his son, with a car and threatening to kill John.

His trial was being prosecuted by Assistant Prosecutor James Flynn.

The Jersey Journal

Saturday November 19 1983. P 3

Article: Prongay Arraignment this month

"Robert Prongay of North Bergen, indicted on charges of arson involving his ex-wife's home, aggravated assault, making terroristic threats and disobeying a court order, faces arraignment in Superior Court later this month.

Prongay according to a Hudson County Grand Jury indictment handed up to Superior Court Judge Burrell Ives Humphreys, is accused of causing explosions at the Charles Court home of his former wife, Ellen, Aug, 9 and Oct 31, attempting to run her and their 16-year old son down with his auto, threatening the boy's life and disobeying Judge J, Leonard Hornstein."

Prongay arraignment this month

Robert Prongay of North Bergen, indicted on charges of arson involving his ex-wife's home, aggravated assault, making terroristic threats and disobeying a court order, faces arraignment in Superior Court later this month.

Prongay, according to a Hudson County Grand Jury indictment handed up to Superior Court Judge Burrell Ives Humphreys, is accused of causing explosions at the Charles Court home of his former wife, Ellen, Aug. 9 and Oct. 31, attempting to run her and their 16-year-old son down with his auto, threatening the boy's life and disobeying Judge J. Leonard Hornstein.

Newspaper clipping from The Jersey Journal. Saturday. November 19th, 1983. Page 3

The Jersey Journal.

Wednesday, November 9, 1983. P. 6

Article: Charged with fireworks.

"A North Bergen man is scheduled to appear in Central Judicial Processing Court today for fireworks possession according to police. Police said yesterday they had to break down the door when Robert Prongay, 37 of Tonnelle Avenue refused to allow officers to enter his residence late Monday night.

Prongay was indicted on charges of aggravated assault, arson, terroristic threats and contempt of court. North Bergen police alleged they found a cache of fireworks after entering the home and charged Prongay with possession of fireworks."

Newspaper clipping from The Jersey Journal. Wednesday. November 9th, 1983. Page 6.

Police

Stabbing victim found

A Union City man, identified as Alejandro Tamayo, 31, was found early today with multiple stab wounds lying on the sidewalk at Bergenline Avenue and 26th Street, Union City police reported. Police said Tamayo was taken to Riverside General Hospital, Secaucus, where he was reported in stable condition with wounds of the head, chest and arms.

Caught in parked car

A 15-year-old Jersey City boy was caught inside a car owned by a New York City man on Palisade Avenue late last night, police reported. The officers, on routine patrol, spotted the youth going through the glove compartment in the vehicle, police said.

Charged with fireworks

A North Bergen man is scheduled to appear in Central Judicial Processing Court today for fireworks possession according to police. Police said yesterday they had to break down the door when Robert Prongay, 37, of Tonnelle Avenue refused to allow offices to enter his residence late Monday night. Prongay was indicted on charges of aggravated assault, arson, terroristic threats and contempt of court. North Bergen police alleged they found a cache of fireworks after entering the home and charged Prongay with possession of fireworks.

Assaulted, robbed

Victor Nunez, 61, of Jersey City, was assaulted by two men and robbed of $33 on Bostwick Avenue last night, police reported.

Mugged on elevator

Maria Ramos, 35, of Jersey City, was robbed at knifepoint of $150 and her husband, Rafael, 45, assaulted by three men on an elevator in a building in the Duncan housing project last night, police reported. Mr. Ramos was treated for a cut of the lower lip at the Medical Center.

Robbed of $85

Two men assaulted Kenneth Ganous, 38, of Jersey City, and robbed him of $85 at Audubon Avenue and Kennedy Boulevard last night, police reported.

14

Operation Iceman
&
Richards Arrest

1981 - 1986

"Richard Kuklinski is one of the most dangerous criminals we have ever come across in this state.

He murdered by guns, he murdered by strangulation, he murdered by putting poison on victims' food. He did all of this, while at the same time exhibiting a normal placid family existence"

Robert J. Carroll Asst. Attorney General 1992

The Investigation

The name Kuklinski had been popping up for the police over several years. It had seemed to be connected to a number of crimes from car theft and burglary to missing persons and murder. He was noted in some crimes as only Big Rich, The Pollack or RK. In others his proper name had been given.

One of these early investigations began in March of 1981. Lieutenant Pat Kane of the New Jersey state police was asked to investigate some burglaries that had been happening in the local area.

After spending time looking into the crimes, he had discovered they were all linked to the same 5 people. These crimes had been occurring in 3 different counties over a span of about a year. One of the names that came up often was Richard Kuklinski, this name could be linked to 40 burglaries and 20 stolen vehicles.

Pat Kane wasn't the only one who had noticed the name Kuklinski. Henry Winters, a police officer working in Huntingdon, Pennsylvania was investigating a missing persons case. During his investigation into Louis Masgays disappearance, he had spoken to the wife and son of Louis. Both of them had said that Louis was on his way to meet Richard Kuklinski before he went missing.

After passing this information on to the New Jersey state police Winters wasn't able to do much else. He would chase it up every now and then, but the case seemed to hit a brick wall. It had been a year and Louis was still missing, the only thing that had been found, was his abandoned vehicle.

By this point Pat Kane had been looking into Richard Kuklinski for a while. He had noted that Richards name came up in the missing persons investigation in Huntington. By this point the man had been missing for well over a year.

Since then Pat Kane had information to suggest that Kuklinski was also involved with the murder of George Malliband. Just like Louis, one of the last people George was seen with before he disappeared was Richard Kuklinski. Pat knew there was a more sinister connection.

Pat Kane spent the next few years gathering intelligence and evidence, eventually putting together a case in the early months of 1982. He presented his findings to the Jury and was given his indictments against the 5 individuals. The charges totalling to 153 counts against all five men.

The hunt had begun for the burglary gang, the first to be arrested was Percy House. Once House was in custody, he told all to get a plea deal. The police needed to find the missing members before they could get convictions, so the search was on.

Louis Masgays body had been recovered, after it was dumped along the side of a road some 15 months after he had been reported missing. During the autopsy on his body, they had discovered that Louis had been frozen and at the time was still defrosting. It was also noted that the clothing that Louis Masgay had on, was the exact same clothing he was reported missing in. Suggesting he had died in close proximity to being reported missing by his family. This rang alarm bells, the last person he was reported to be with was Richard. Due to this Richard had earned the nickname of the Iceman from law enforcement working the Masgay case little did they know this nickname would stick.

It had been nearly 4 years since Pat Kane had begun his investigation and he was no closer to finding Kuklinski. He had plenty of circumstantial evidence that placed Kuklinski directly at the scene of many suspected crimes, but he had nothing solid on him. With burglary charges against him, missing persons being linked to him and affiliation to at least 3 murders Richard was a high priority.

Pat knew that to catch Richard they would need to play his game. After much deliberation Pat decided he had only one option, to carry out an undercover operation and catch Kuklinski in the act, red handed. There would be no way he could get out of that one. After speaking to other law enforcement agencies, it was agreed that an undercover operation was needed.

Working together, these agencies came up with a plan to infiltrate Kuklinski and get the evidence they needed to make an arrest and a conviction. A sting operation was put together called, Operation Iceman. This undercover operation lasted roughly 2 years.

Operation Iceman

It was nearly 1985, and Richard was suspected of multiple murders (among other crimes). Various Law Enforcement agencies knew he was directly linked to these crimes, however, didn't have enough solid evidence to prove it in order to make an arrest and a conviction. Pat Kane had pieced together what he could over the last 4 years of his investigation, now he just needed the man himself.

Several missing and deceased persons had been linked to Kuklinski over the years. Most were rumoured to of been with him shortly before they were killed or disappeared. The police knew if they didn't catch Richard soon more bodies would show up and more people would go missing. The operation was set up and the wheels were put into motion.

It was headed and organised by Pat Kane, with help from prosecutor Bob Caroll. The plan was to use two undercover agents to lure Kuklinski in, under the guise that he was being hired to carry out a hit. Everything they did would need to be recorded which would mean a wire would need to be worn at all times, and surveillance of Richards movements would be vital.

For this to be done right the best agent for the job had to be used. Richard wasn't stupid nor was he very trusting. The slightest inkling that something was off with the situation could scare Richard away. They would need someone who would fit easily into Richards world, someone who could talk the talk and walk the walk confidently. It was recommended by others in the police force that Special agent Dominick Polifrone would be the perfect man for this job. He had years of experience with men just like Richard and was a very convincing criminal. Dominick knew this was a risky job but also knew he was capable. He was given the task to be the one to infiltrate Richard and get as much evidence as he could of Richards crimes.

To be able to carry this out they needed a target for Richard, someone who would be the victim of the fabricated hit. Someone just as convincing as Dominick. Agent Paul Smith was drafted in for this job. His role was to play a spoilt rich kid who would be the unknowing target of Dominicks planned hit.

With Dominick posing as a mafia associated drug and gun dealer called Michael Dominick Provenzano. And Paul Smith as the intended target they had a plan of action. The next part would be the most difficult, getting their foot in the door of Kuklinskis world.

Knowing some of the places Richard had been known to frequent their first stop was Phil Solimenes store. With a bit of legal persuasion, the store was infiltrated by the undercover ATF agent. Phil had agreed that Dominick could use his store as an initial point of contact. They knew Richard used the store often so it would be a good place to get Dominick introduced to him.

The facade was to build up a working relationship with Richard and gain his trust via criminal activity. Dominick used his contact with local informants who personally knew Kuklinski to do this. The task force knew these types of operations were slow going and patience was a must, however it seemed as though no matter what they tried they couldn't get an introduction to Richard.

After a year and a half into the investigation Dominick still had not been introduced to Kuklinski. Becoming impatient he approached his informant in the Paterson store, and pushed him to arrange a meeting with Kuklinski. He had tried this multiple times before but had nothing come from it. This was frustrating Dominick, if they didn't make headway soon the whole thing would be called off and he would have wasted the last year. Dominick didn't like the thought of failing.

It was explained to Dom that Richard was not a man you could just approach and introduce someone to. That he was easily "spooked" (Bruno. 1993) and to have patience. Those who knew Richard at the store referred to Richard as 'the devil himself', this nickname was given to him for a reason. Richard was not someone you could just call up and have a friendly chat with. Dominick, although impatient, understood his introduction would need to have purpose.

Polifrones first contact with Richard Kuklinski was due to Richard needing pure cyanide to carry out a murder. Richard had spoken to Dominicks informant on the phone asking if him, if he knew of a guy that could get drugs for him. At this point Dominick was recommended as the man to go to, and a meeting was set up between them.

Richard was told Dominicks last name was Provenzano and that he was mafia affiliated. He was under the impression that Dominick did most of his business in downtown New York and that he was a connected guy. So, Richard figured he would be able to get his hands on the things he needed. After all, these connected guys could get their hands on most things.

Dominick and Kuklinski met up for coffee to discuss the transaction. This was Dominick's moment to secure a working relationship with Kuklinski. This was the moment he had been waiting for. After a discussion about drugs, Richard seemed to feel comfortable enough to ask Dominick if he could get his hands-on pure cyanide. Slightly taken aback by Richards upfront request, Dominick agreed and told Richard he had a guy he knew that could probably get it.

In response to Richards request, Dominick asked Richard if he could get hold of military grade weapons. He told Richard he needed these for the IRA and that they were good customers of his who would pay big bucks for the right weapons. Dominick said this knowing Richard could not refuse large sums of money. After a brief discussion about the finer details of the jobs they had for one another, Richard asked how he could get hold of Dominick to let him know when everything was ready. They exchanged pager numbers and Dominick told Richard to keep in touch with him to make arrangements once the deal was sorted out.

Unknown to Dominick at that time the pager number he was given by Kuklinski was one of two pagers that Kuklinski used. Richard had a pager for friends, work associates, and family and then another he would give to his potential victims. Dominick was given the latter.

Once a relationship was established via the initial meeting, Dominick was able to approach Kuklinski to freely discuss the hit job he had for Richard. Dominick had agreed to provide the cyanide needed to carry it out. After a couple of meetings the day finally came for the sting to come to a head.

Kuklinski was under the impression he was being hired to kill a cocaine dealer, a spoiled rich kid with nothing better to do. Richard was told by Dom that the target would have copious amounts of cash on their persons. The plan was for Kuklinski to poison the target, then take the money.

The day had come for the transaction of cyanide it was the 17th of December 1986. Everyone involved with Operation Iceman knew that this day was make or break, if they didn't get it exactly right it could mean Richard would slip out of their hands. With this in mind the pressure was on to get it right.

On the day of his arrest, Richard had met up early in the day with Dom to collect the cyanide that was to be used in the hit. The first part of the plan was going well, Richard took the cyanide ready to put it to use.

After picking up what he believed was pure cyanide he knew he needed to test it out, something Dominick had not accounted for. Richard tested the cyanide on an animal. After there was no response Richard realised it was not cyanide and became frustrated. The surveillance team his reaction and knew the plan was off.

Instead of continuing with the plan for the hit he decided to go home, annoyed that Dominick had wasted his time and money. Richards mind was doing somersaults at the thought he'd been conned, he would have to make Dominick pay for this one way or another.

Due to this change of plan the team of undercover agents knew the arrest had to be made quickly in case Richard decided to retaliate and kill Dominick for his deception. By this point they had Richard on tape confessing to other murders to Dominick, they had tapes with Richard breaking down how he kills and what his preferred methods are. He had disclosed a lot of information they had not expected to get on record. They knew him collecting what he thought was pure cyanide would be enough evidence of intent to arrest and convict Kuklinski for attempted murder. Along with the other bits of evidence they had against him they felt they would have a strong enough case. One strong enough to at least charge him with attempted murder and conspiracy to murder.

A roadblock was then set up on his street a few hours after the meeting to collect the cyanide. They did this to trap him to make the arrest as quickly as possible before Richard could come after any of them. As Richard drove down his road to take Barbara to the doctors he was blocked in and police surrounded his car.

Kuklinski is a tall and stocky man with a lot of natural strength, the officers that arrested him described him as difficult to take down due to his size and stature. Pat Kane said getting the handcuffs on him was a struggle.

The operation, although not always going to plan had resulted in the arrest of Kuklinski for conspiracy to murder among other charges. Finally, they had him, and they had charges that would stick, recordings that were more than incriminating to hold him.

But this information alone wouldn't be enough to convict him for all he had done. There were still unsolved cases of murder linked to Kuklinski. The evidence from Operation Iceman couldn't be used in all of the crimes he had committed. The sole reason that the police needed to take him down in the way they had was because Richard was so good at evading them. But now he was caught they could piece together all the other evidence they had on him and get convictions for as much of it as possible.

The Trials and Evidence

Richard's downfall was not the admissions to Polifrone caught on tape, nor was it the purchase of the fake cyanide from undercover police. It was killing those he was associated to, such as, George Malliband, Louis Masgay and Gary Smith.

The undercover operation helped to solidify the evidence of these other crimes and meant they were able to arrest him on conspiracy to murder. On the basis that, Richard thought he was buying pure cyanide. Therefore, clear intent to commit murder could be identified.

There was no real case with the recordings obtained via operation Iceman alone. As far as the courts would be concerned those admissions wouldn't be enough to get a conviction. They could be passed off as lies or mindless bragging with no real basis in truth. The arresting officers knew this and knew without other evidence they had no case, they had essentially wasted time.

Although they got a conviction, the undercover operation was not a success on the whole. It had taken Dominick a lot of time to get near to Kuklinski, and even when he did there was talk of terminating the operation because it wasn't progressing. This was something Dominick refuted, insisting he could get Richard to buy what he thought was cyanide. It was a good thing Dominick had been persistent, even though in the back of his mind he knew Richard might be plotting to kill him too. He didn't let this anxiety get the better of him, he was determined to achieve what he said he would.

With the deal set up and done they had their man, Richard had bought the lie and taken the bait. That said once Richard had come to the realisation that the cyanide he had obtained through Polifrone was a dud, he had started to plan to take out Dominick instead. This was the reason they had to act quickly and make the arrest. Had they not done this the undercover police and ATF agents would be the next targets of the devil himself.

The cases of victims such as Malliband, provided documentation linking Kuklinski to the victims, and witnesses who saw Richard with victims before they disappeared. In many cases the victims told loved ones of their association to him and why they were meeting up with him. It was this type of testimony from some 34 witnesses that took down the Iceman Kuklinski in court.

It was told to the court in reports how Malliband expressed to more than one person that he was worried something may happen to him. That if anything did happen to him it was over the money he was carrying with him.

The killings associated with the members of his Breaking and Entering gang provided evidence of calls made to and from the motel where Gary and Daniel were hiding out. Calls that went directly to Kuklinskis home number. They showed direct links to the victims. Which could then be used as evidence in the courts. Evidence the police needed.

Barbara Deppner a state witness told all when the police attended her house over a routine noise complaint. She ended up panicking and telling them everything she knew about the death of Gary Smith, directly placing Richard at the crime as the perpetrator of the murder. She later testified in court against Richard.

She testified during the trial of Gary Smiths murder, that Percy told her after his arrest to relay a message to Richard Kuklinski, "to send Gary Smith to Florida because he was very shaky and, if the cops caught him, he could send everyone to jail" - Barbara Deppner (1988)

The testimony of those such as Percy House gave them more evidence, Percy House had admitted to the discussion with Barbara in prison where he was alleged to have, 'ordered the killings of Smith and Deppner' – Neal Frank (1988) 'go to Florida' was a code used by the gang to talk about those that needed to be killed, if someone was sent to Florida it meant their time was up.

Due to the mounting witnesses, the evidence collected by the various law enforcement agencies and the undercover operation, Richard was finally captured by the state and bought to justice. It took the efforts of multiple people and many years of investigation to do this. But it was worth it for the officers involved, who had taken a dangerous man off the streets, hopefully for good.

By the end of his Trials and many confessions Richard would be incarcerated for at least the next 111 years. Pleading guilty to the murders he had committed and later confessing to others he was linked to, ensured he would never be released from prison.

15

Motives, Violence And Drives

"I would move heaven, hell, and anything in between to get to you. You wouldn't be safe anywhere if I was mad at you."

Motive for murder

The murders he committed through contracts and cons is solely monetary. He stated in court that they were "just business" nothing more. In interviews when describing some of these murders he is emotionless and very matter of fact. There is nothing to indicate that he had any other motive than a monetary one.

The acts of murder he committed against people like George Malliband had more than just a cash incentive. These were reactive, based on his perceived personal slights and situation. The need to regain control of a situation where Richard perceived the person as a threat to either his family or himself. If he felt as though they would flip and go to the police and tell all, he would act how he deemed appropriate. His resolution to this problem was to kill them.

He saw these killings as a practical necessity. To maintain control of the situation, he reacts almost instantly eliminating the threat while keeping power. At times he has murdered out of disgust, disgust at the person or again at something they had implied or said.

The murders of his gang associates were instrumental and committed solely for self-preservation. He gained no money from these and no form of pleasure or satisfaction. He was just "tying up loose ends" as he put it, to stop anything leading back to him. His goal was to remove the witnesses of his crimes.

It's clear Richards motives for his crimes vary, however, the majority were motivated by greed. Specifically, large sums of cash.

He would set up fake deals/business transactions and then kill the person when they showed up with the money. "He would set up business deals and when the people arrived with their side of the deal, with their part of the bargain, he would kill them. " Attorney General W. Cary Edwards (1986)

The victims he targeted for this were associated to hired hits or cons. He did not know them personally, or at least not well enough that they would consider him a friend. In some cases, he would have to get them into situations where he was alone or in a confined space with them. Enough to be able to execute the murder.

An example of this can be seen in the case of Paul Hoffman. Hoffman was only a distant associate/connection. He had no personal interaction with him other than arranging the exchange of drugs for money. Yet he was lured easily by the promise of a great deal.

His murders had a purpose. According to him that purpose being driven by the want for money and the urgency to not be caught by law enforcement. Or to protect his family. He would kill people he felt would expose him or had the means to expose him.

Violence

Richard uses violence and the choice to murder in a variety of ways. There are times the violent acts he commits are calculated and controlled, they have a goal and instrumental purpose. At other times the violence may be impulsive, and erratic based on primal reactions of anger and rage, with no real thought or planning going into them.

As he got older his crimes progressed and his behaviour became more violent. He developed ways of using violence to get what he wanted and would decide when murder was necessary. Some of his violent crimes ended in murder, others were more strategic and violence was used to keep control rather than to kill.

For example, not all of Richards violent outbursts towards his family were impulsive or reactive based. At times Richard uses instrumental violence as a means to maintain control over his family.

His ultimate goal is to stop them from leaving him and he is driven by this. He uses his outbursts and sudden bouts of violence to do this. Richard knows it will make his family fearful of leaving him and act as a deterrent.

He demonstrated this in the early 1960's when Barbara tried to end their relationship and he stabbed her. Richard is calm and stern and says to Barbara, "That's an object lesson. Don't ever try to leave me". He could have killed her if he had wanted to, but instead used it as a warning to her not to underestimate him.

Barbara was often the target of this strategy, he would use violence towards Barbara in front of the children. His children don't discuss being physically abused by Richard, but they do talk about the lasting psychological impact of them seeing him abuse their mother. They were scared for her on many occasions.

Although his children never reported physical abuse towards them, he has used techniques of emotional manipulation and threats of violence to instil fear into them. He explicitly told his daughter that he would have to kill the children if Barbara ever tried to leave him.

There are times his wife and daughters describe him as having weeks where he would be depressed and lock himself away, he would often smash and break things. If they interrupted him or intervened it could get worse, he had threatened their lives before on occasion.

Richard is perfectly capable of killing his wife and children but chooses not to react this way. He has control of his choices and can hold back if he chooses to do so. In these situations, he does hold back. Others outside of his family unit have not been so lucky, his rage toward them is almost instant and seemingly uncontrollable.

From a young age Richard was shown how to use violence to get what he wanted or to deal with people who went against him. His father Stanley essentially gave him this skill which was then reinforced by his experiences with society. The bullies in his area were feared and respected by their peers, they would do whatever they wanted because they had control. If any of the other kids challenged that control, they were targeted and beaten with seemingly no negative consequences. When Richard himself began to use violence as a way to gain, he suffered little to no consequences either. Helping to solidify that violence was a way to get what you wanted in life.

Drives

Richard was not driven to kill through any perverse sexual desire. He did not have a specific type of person or appearance that would trigger his desire to kill either.

His drives were associated to his personal experiences and perceptions, the desire for self-preservation and the preservation of the family unit. Also, to maintain control of that. Richard seemingly had no addictions; he did not drink, take drugs, or gamble. Nor did he frequent sex workers or stripclubs.

There have been times he claimed he had killed based on his emotional drives, reactivity, and feelings of disgust for the person. An example of this is Robert Prongay aka Mister Softee. He was personally associated to him and attributes much of his knowledge on explosives, poisons, and body disposal to him.

When he talks of Robert, it is somewhat in admiration of his skills however, Richard does state that Mr Softee, although deadly, was also crazy. He claimed he shot and killed Mister Softee after he had approached Richard about carrying out a hit on his ex-wife and their children. This was an emotionally led reaction, Richard was disgusted by the notion that Robert would kill his own family and reacted almost instantaneously. He was driven by this internal disgust.

It is possible that this reminded him of the destructive and abusive nature his parents had towards him as a child, coupled with the fact he held his own children and family in the highest regard. They were the most important thing to him. In his mind the very reason he was involved in this criminal lifestyle was to cater to his family. To make sure they did not grow up in poverty and pain like he had. Going to great lengths to make sure nothing negatively affected that. In his eyes he could justify some of his actions regarding those he had killed. For example, if he felt that a person had made a threat against his family. In other cases, he had no justification, only the fact he had wanted the money.

He did have drives to harm others unprovoked and unnecessarily. This can be seen when he tortures or hurts animals. This drive and initial act would excite him, but he said eventually that feeling would lead to disgust. He was not clear if that disgust was at himself and his actions, or if he was disgusted by the remains of his actions.

He also explained that it made him feel powerful, confident and in control. These are things Richard said he lacked during his childhood and would often feel out of control of in his own life. Resentful and angry at those who he saw as having power over him. He learned from an incredibly young age that power and control can be achieve through brute force.

16

Style, Methods
and
Weapons

"If there is a will, there is a way my friend"

Most of Richard's crimes were premeditated rather than impulsive the majority of the time, but also disorganised. His choice in method varied, dependant on the person, his relationship with them and the situation around the murder. This was also reflected in his weapon choices.

In some respects, he went to great lengths to cover up his crimes, such as storing a body in a freezer for two years. In order to distort time of death and sabotage the investigation. But then in other crimes he left obvious forensic evidence such as shell casings, and carelessly dumping bodies. The crimes were planned, yet at times sloppy in execution. In some cases, he seemed to be led by impatience, using more than one weapon to ensure the victim was dead. E.g., using cyanide as a primary weapon and then strangulation as a secondary weapon.

Some of Richards victims were people that he could get up close and personal with. People who somewhat trusted him. He knew many of them personally enough for them to be around him alone and be close to him while eating and drinking. They were comfortable enough with this, despite some of them knowing that he had killed others using poison.

As time went on Richard seemed to become more complacent in covering up his crimes. For example, previously he had gone to great lengths to dispose and hide bodies. However, in the case of Gary Smith, he made no real effort to cover the crime at all, he merely stuffed the body under the motel bed "for someone else to find" - Kuklinski (1992). He did this despite people knowing he had a working relationship with Gary Smith. In previous murders he had been known to carefully wrap the body and either store it somewhere, or make it look like the person died of natural causes.

This laziness could have also been a symptom of his confidence and arrogance. He had spent so much time 'getting away with it' that he may have felt untouchable in regards to getting caught. So over time became complacent and assuming he was too clever to be caught.

Weapons

The choice of weapon would depend on the job he was doing. His methods varied from beating, strangulation, stabbing, shooting to poisoning.

When he was out on the street, he carried 3 guns and a hunting knife. The number of guns he carried was down to the fact that he said a gun had jammed on him before. He had no back up weapon so had to use his initiative to kill the person. This wasn't a situation he wanted to be in again, so always had a backup gun from then on (a display of his level of experience in his work).

He kept a Derringer in each pocket and a revolver strapped to his ankle. He owned a 22 Calibre Black & White Derringer, which was recovered by Law Enforcement, reinforcing these claims. He also tended to use shotguns from time to time.

He used cyanide, on occasions, in either powder or liquid form. He would use a spray bottle to administer it, or it would be put into the victim's food. He preferred this method overall.

Richard has used strangulation as a method of killing. This is not his first choice in method and is a technique he uses as a back-up. He doesn't carry a ligature as a weapon, there is no evidence that this weapon is a premeditated choice. The times he has used one it was an item already present and to hand at the primary crime scene.

In tapes that were recorded during the undercover investigation on Kuklinski, he can be heard saying to agent Polifrone that he prefers to use clean methods. "The only thing I don't understand. Don't you use a fuckin' piece of iron to get rid of these fuckin' people, or do you use this fuckin' cyanide?" -Polifrone (1986). Richard replies, "Why be messy? You do it, nice and calm." - Kuklinski (1986).

This distaste for being messy is also apparent during his HBO interviews, when he talks about using tools such as chainsaws or tire irons. He explains they were never his first choice and ultimately his last, that he tried to avoid using those kinds of methods to kill.

This would make poisoning his preferred method, secondary would be shooting the target/victim, leaving strangulation being the third. These are all quick and efficient methods, creating situations where Richard can leave the crime scene quickly, leaving minimal mess.

Poisoning, in some cases, may even mean he does not have to deal with the clean-up and disposal of the body, making his job much easier.

These types of crimes require a person to have built the trust of their target, or at least have some sort of purpose to be around them that would not arouse suspicion. Richard would need to be up close and personal with them most of the time. In cases where he has poisoned a person's food, that person would need to have enough trust of him to leave food or have food around him.

In cases of shooting, Richard does this at close range, he carries back up guns and shows clear pre-planning of how the crime will be carried out. He will often use the facade of business and drug deals as a rouse to lure targets to a location. This means he has full access to the person, and they are alone in close proximity to one another. This enables Richard to dominate the situation and keep control.

(During surveillance Richard would show up at locations hours early to scope out who was there he was very cautious)

Disposing bodies was based on what purpose he had for them, whether he wanted them to be found or not would make a difference. If he wasn't bothered about them being found he would just dump them anywhere he deemed suited. If he didn't want them to be found he would take extra precautions.

He has no pattern or routine when it comes to killing, methods, styles. He will act as he feels in the situation he is presented with.

17

Personality traits
&
Emotions

"I am probably the loneliest person in the world ... I've lost everything I ever cared for. Everything I ever wanted. It's down the toilet. Since there is no love in my life, I must have something to replace it, so I replaced it with hate." Kuklinski

Dissociation is one of the main aspect of Richards coping mechanisms. It is one of the things that has given him this ability to switch off from the crimes he commits and detach himself from any feeling of guilt or remorse.

This was learned via early trauma in life. He talks about not thinking about certain things so that he does not have to feel them. He appears to have gained this skill during the various beatings his father would give him. He described, that while his father carried out those beatings he learned to, "think of something else" Kuklinski (1992) to distract himself from what was happening and to nullify the pain from it.

This would suggest that he does feel emotion, discomfort, and possible guilt. However only when he thinks about them and the implications.

This means he can possibly identify with his victims, or at least how they may have felt during that moment but chooses not to, so he doesn't have to face the implications of his actions. The motive for this disassociation appears to be to evade hurting himself in the process of remembering and identifying emotionally with the moment. Selfish acts regardless.

During his interviews with HBO, he was diagnosed by Dr Park Dietz who is a Forensic Psychiatrist. After speaking with Richard over a few sessions Dietz identified that Richard had:

- Anti-social Personality Disorder, with Traits of factor 1 & 2 psychopathy.

- Narcissistic Personality Disorder - self-serving, egotistical, constant need for admiration, lack of empathy.
- Paranoid Personality Disorder.

The first two diagnostics seem fitting and reflect Richards personality. Historically there is evidence of his current and past behaviours that clearly identify issues such as antisocial and narcissistic traits.

He displayed signs of conduct disorder as a teenager, starting out with truancy and moving onto theft, these antisocial behaviours then developed into more vicious acts of actual harm to living things. Beginning with harming animals and progressing to harming people. This became steadily worse as he got older, initially he would feel bad about the violence he had carried out on others, even disgusted at himself at times. This would fade eventually as he became increasingly conditioned to such acts, they began to bother him less and less.

His attitude and personality developed into a very self-serving one, his ultimate goals became to fulfil his own needs, no matter the cost to others. He began to have a very entitled look upon the world, where he was determined to make the world pay for the suffering he went through as a child. He hated being told no and would do whatever he could to avoid it, even if it meant hurting someone.
His size and stature played a key role in his ability to dominate so easily, making getting what he wanted even easier. This only fed into the narcissistic aspects of his personality, inflating his sense of self. In his own mind he had become the ultimate man's man, someone nobody could mess with. The way those in his life would obey him only reinforced the belief that he couldn't be taken down.

Although he did not score particularly high on the HARE PCL-R test he does have clear traits of both Factor 1 & 2 Psychopathy. Which he seems to utilise interchangeably depending on the situation he is put into.

He was diagnosed by Dr Deitz as having Paranoid Personality disorder. However, this is debatable and has been contested by other medical professionals.

For the Paranoid diagnosis to be accurate, the paranoid episodes would need to occur independently of any crime being committed. The paranoia would need to be seen occurring with those in his life who are not criminally involved with him.

It appears from the evidence and information available that Richards paranoia was mostly linked to his criminal behaviour rather than every aspect of his life. It is normal for a person who lives illegitimately to be paranoid about being found out and suspecting ulterior motives in other criminals. This wouldn't be deemed as a personality-based disorder but rather a symptom of his lifestyle.

Someone who truly suffered this disorder would have it consistently manifest in multiple situations throughout their lifetime, not just in specific circumstances, much like Richard's seemed to have been. His paranoid episodes are mostly linked with the idea that people he is involved with criminally can expose him. Which, in reflection, would be perfectly normal things to be paranoid about in that situation. There is no honour among thieves, as they say, so the idea that these people could turn on him to save themselves is not that far-fetched. There was a real possibility that these people could take him down if they decided to speak to Law Enforcement.

If we look at the victims of his paranoid based behaviours, we see a pattern forming. The moment he suspects a person could flip on him he eradicates them. The notion that dead men tell no tales is prevalent here. Each of these victims were close to him, they all knew information about him that could potentially get him killed or arrested. Had we seen Richard displaying behaviours or acting paranoid in other situations in his life this diagnosis may be a more fitting one.

Emotions

Richard likes to come across as emotionless but that is far from truth. He is an emotional man, but he does not regulate his emotions like a normal person would. He states he does not feel any way about killing but also contradicts himself later in his interview tapes.

He feels anger and frustration and is somewhat led by these emotions, finding them difficult to control at times, they seem to be very reactive for him. We see this in some of his crimes and sometimes with those he personally knows. In these instances, he's reacted based upon emotions of anger, which is a trait linked with factor 2 Psychopathy. This high Neuroticism can cause explosive and chaotic behaviours leading to erratic disorganised outbursts of things like sudden rage.

But it is on record that he had control of this and chose to react that way, it wasn't that he couldn't stop himself it is because he didn't want to. He would use his outbursts and rages with Barbara with purpose to get what he wanted. She has recalled times during his episodes where he would be yelling and hitting her completely enraged and the phone would ring. He would suddenly stop and go calm before answering the phone and chatting like nothing had happened, then as soon as that phone went click, he would start yelling and going crazy again.

On the flip side, Richards demeanour changes when he is dealing with someone, he has no personal connection to. When it is a stranger, he is able to remain emotionally disconnected and unreactive, he focuses only on the task at hand and the outcome. This callous and cold approach is something seen in a person with Factor 1 Psychopathy.

Those with factor 1 Psychopathy are believed to have decreased or delayed brain functioning regarding attention, processing fear, and connecting emotions with actions and language. This can be seen especially when looking at their comprehension of compassion, remorse, and empathy. It is because of this interference in cognition that they can be callous, self-serving, and seemingly evade feelings of guilt.

This can also make them come across as fearless, it has been identified that this type of fearlessness is also linked with brain functioning that can be found in those with Psychopathy. "Higher-order cognitive processes moderate the fear deficits of psychopathic individuals. These findings suggest that psychopaths' diminished reactivity to fear stimuli, and emotion-related cues more generally, reflect idiosyncrasies in attention that limit their processing of peripheral information." - Newman, J *et al* (2009).

Although there is not a complete disconnect from emotion, it means that a person with factor 1 psychopathy is limited in emotional regulation and understanding. Richard does seem to have clear traits of someone with factor 1 psychopathy, he has the ability to disconnect himself with his victims emotionally. He does not seem to acknowledge the impact of his actions on them nor does he seem to care.

This is most prevalent in those he killed that he was loosely associated to. In his interview tapes he gives the impression he is consciously aware of his ability to disconnect himself with specific acts. In fact, that he does so through choice, so he does not have to feel emotions. Suggesting that he does have comprehension of empathy and compassion and chooses when he should apply it and why.

He states that the only reason he does not feel emotion for his victims is because he just does not think about it. But if he does think about it, then it upsets him, so he just does not. This shows that although he is able to disconnect himself in the moment of the killing, he is not emotionally detached from it completely, as would first be assumed.

This is a learned skill that most likely developed as he was growing up. He doesn't like to be upset or have those feelings, so uses techniques to avoid them. The skill of managing positive and negative emotions is a learned one. It is possible that Richard's learned ways of coping with these emotions is not to confront them, but to instead suppress them, giving the impression he is emotionless.

During his interviews he is asked "Are there any murders that haunt you?", Richard replies, "No murders haunt me. Nothing. I do not think about it. That's why it's hard for me to tell you. In order for me to be able to tell you when something happened, I'd have to think about it. If I think about it, it would wind up hurting me. So I don't, I don't think about it" - Richard Kuklinski (1992).

However, in contrast to this, he also seems to be able to indirectly relate to the suffering of others if he is emotionally connected to them. He feels personal loss and pain when he talks about his family. He is clearly emotionally affected by that. He attempts to suppress this during his interviews; however, it can be seen in various facial tells and body language, along with his construct of language.

At one stage he is questioned about his regrets in life, he starts to talk about his ex-wife Barbara and their children and what he has put them through. Seemingly identifying with the pain he has caused them. At this point he becomes very emotional and the pain he is feeling can be seen outwardly in his facial expressions and breaks in speech.

He starts to cry and seems somewhat embarrassed about it. He sees crying as emasculating and shameful, this was possibly learned behaviour that stems from his childhood. The feelings of shame and emasculation causes him to try to supress and ignore certain feelings. Not outwardly reacting to them, causing him to become numb and emotionally unresponsive over time.

Although this sudden show of emotion seems compassionate, it cannot be ruled out that the only reason he feels this emotion is because of the more selfish aspects. The idea that if it hurt him, it must have hurt them (typical of a person who is self-serving, it is only relatable if they feel it too). This is not so much identifying directly with the victims, but rather indirectly through his own perceived pain and loss.

In 2001 Richard talks about some of the early violent offences he committed during an interview. He talks about situations where he had gotten into fights and beaten people. He speaks specifically about a time when he was a young man. He was in a bar playing pool and got into a disagreement with another man. They went outside to fight where Richard just unleashed blow after blow upon the man with his pool cue.

Richard realised he had hit the man too many times and he had succumbed to his injuries and died. Richard said once he calmed down and realised he felt "very bad" about it and it "upset him", because he didn't mean to hurt him that badly. He had no intention of killing him but had got carried away. He said this upset him a lot at the time. Although when he discusses this moment on camera his face remains expressionless. The emotion and upset he felt that day was not projected using his expression, but only his words which remained very matter of fact.

By the latter stages of Richards life he was conditioned not to react to such things in an emotional or expressive way. Which can account for the seemingly blank response to this event. Although he is speaking about it upsetting him, being able to emotively express that by that late point in his life, wouldn't be something Richard could do. He has learned how to detach and disassociate himself from those things, so that he doesn't have to deal with emotions or the negative feelings that come with such acts of violence.

It appears he interchanges between factor 1 and factor 2 psychopathy based on the circumstance and connection with the victim. Richard started out life being the victim and ultimately ended his life being the abuser. He talks about his childhood consisting of being beaten, ridiculed, and bullied by others. The feeling of despair and lack of control overwhelmed him at times.

The desire to get that control back and make others suffer like he did, grew over time manifesting into a frustration and rage. The hatred that built up over time for both his mother and father. The feelings of abandonment and loneliness, coupled with fear, meant Richard developed and learned coping skills built around being hurt, unloved and afraid. Regarding people like Richard, who are pathological or psychopathic, it is often found that the relationship between them and their main care givers, especially the mother are at the forefront of their disorder.

This duration of early life neglect and abuse has been shown to be a contributor to violent and aggressive behaviour later in life. If it is not amended early on it can have devastating implications.

It got to a point where Richard would no longer put up with being a target and a victim. He chose in his eyes to fight back, to become the aggressive one. He describes that being the aggressor and not the victim made him feel excited and he got an adrenaline rush. He enjoyed the feeling of being in control and having the power. He states "that was the day I learned it was better to give than to receive" -Kuklinski (1992)

18

Lying, Embellishment

&

Truth

How do you feel about killing?
"I don't, it doesn't bother me. It doesn't bother
me at all. I don't have a feeling one way or
another"   Kuklinski Conversations with a killer
1992

Richard is aware of what he is doing when it comes to his story telling. He is a smart man; he has learned over time how to mix fact with fiction and make it believable. Richard spent much of his adult life deceiving people, convincingly. One of the reasons his criminal career was able to continue for so long (1949 – 1986) undetected by Law Enforcement is because, he could effectively deceive and evade detection.

Before Richards arrest for the murders he committed, he had only been arrested once in 1958, this was in Jersey City for receiving stolen goods. At the time he was living at 39 Newkirk St Jersey City before he had moved to Dumont. Other than that, he had no record, he would not have been on the police radar as one to keep an eye on.

The same goes with those that knew him as a family man. None of his family knew about Richards behaviours. He had convinced them otherwise. Those who have met Richard and spoken to him personally have said that he is very charming and sure of himself which makes him convincing.

The only people who seemed to have any idea of who the real Richard was, were his criminal associates. He earned nicknames like "Big Rich" and "The Devil Himself" due to this reputation. During the Iceman Operation Dominick had issues initially being introduced to Richard because people were too wary of Kuklinski. They were genuinely anxious of upsetting him in case it had repercussions. This gives an example of the way in which they perceived him. They did not see this friendly approachable family man, that Richard would portray elsewhere. They saw a 6ft4" emotionless killer, a conman, a person who didn't hesitate to remove anyone he saw as a problem.

During the time Anthony Bruno was researching for his book about Kuklinski he would receive letters from Richard. In these letters he would discuss crimes. There was a particularly long letter consisting of 150 pages, breaking down stories of murders he had committed. He ends the letter with "These stories may just be fiction or fact only I know for sure." The monotony of prison and the excitement of having the attention on him makes it easy to see why a man like Richard might decide to lie or embellish.

It's fitting of his personality traits overall. Somewhat habitual behaviour he may have seen as necessary, especially if he has a motive to portray himself in a specific way. This would be the perfect way to solidify that persona and leave behind a trail of curiosity into his case.

When he talks about killings he seems to embellish and can come across as he is lying. He seems to gain pleasure (excitement) from the idea that he is shocking the audience or interviewer and duping them. The idea that he is responsible for 200+ murders as he claims seems more of a baseless claim than a reliable one. Yes, we know he is capable of killing and getting away with it, but such high numbers seem unlikely.

During his recorded interview with Dr Dietz, Richard is directly questioned on the numbers of people he has killed. He does not answer this question in the same manner he has answered previous ones. He is looking for a reaction from the interviewer rather than being honest before he answers. He replies with a question, rather than an answer and tentatively skirts around it.

There are times you see him cover his face and stroke his nose as he speaks about the numbers exceeding 100 people. This is a subconscious attempt at hiding his deception, it's a way to sooth the anxiety of the deception. You see the difference when you observe him during questioning of crimes the public know he has done. He answers more directly without the hesitation and doesn't look for approval, he keeps his hands in place and doesn't attempt to reassure himself. This raises the question why would he want people to think he had killed this many people, what would that achieve? It has to be looked at from Richards perspective to be understood.

The motivation for this could be several things, he could be doing this to gain notoriety and infamy - to a person like Richard such violent and despicable acts show he is to be feared, he is not weak and can-do terrible things if he is crossed. Fear in this instance equates to respect and admiration to the mind of a person like Kuklinski. So, would not be an unusual thing for him to embellish or lie about to garner such a response from people.

It does not seem too farfetched to think that Richard knows he is never getting out of jail and knows his name is somewhat infamous. Regarding the personality traits he has of enjoying power and control it could be said that these claims are false confessions or complete fabrication and lies to inflate his sense of self. This way people will see him as this ruthless killer, a man to be feared and respected. Meaning he will leave a legacy behind as the most dangerous contract killer of all time. He has nothing left to lose in the moments he made these claims during HBO interviews.

He could also be lying to purposely deceive law enforcement, he knows that the interview was for the sole purpose of extracting information from him about his crimes. He is not stupid; he knows that the reason they did it via a television show was to feed into his ego and get him to agree to it. Therefore, he may see it as an opportunity to get some revenge on the police for catching him. By making them waste police time and resources looking into his involvement in crimes that never occurred. Richard has a history of wanting to get revenge on those he feels have done injustices to him. This would be fitting of that aspect of his character.

It could also be down to the fact that Richard is a compulsive liar, from his behaviours historically we know that Richard is an impulsive person who can be led by his compulsions. He may just be lying for the sake of lying, due to the types of personality disorder and abnormalities that he displays in general. Or lastly that he really did carry out all these murders and is in fact one of the worst mass murderers and contract killers in U.S. history.

One way to establish possible truth would be to try to link described acts with unsolved crimes which share similarities in descriptions, one must also be aware that he may have had access to news stories or articles of unsolved crimes of which he could potentially claim. He mixes truth with fiction; due to the crimes we know he has committed it can make it easier for him to lie about or fabricate other crimes.

19

The end of Kuklinski

"I can't change yesterday"

Richard Died in 2006, aged 70, at the time of his death he was still incarcerated in Trenton State prison and he died of natural causes. Leaving behind an infamous trail of destruction. He impacted people's lives and caused the suffering of many, from those that were close to him to those he didn't even know.

Richard's story will always be one to remember, he is a stark reminder that there are those that live among us capable of heinous crimes all in the name of money, control and power. His life and the experiences in it, over time shaped him to become a man who was dangerous, ruthless and greedy.

His parents created an environment where violence, verbal abuse, punishment and religion took priority over affection, fun, forgiveness and most of all love. There was no reassurance for Richard of his safety growing up, he had seen his fathers capabilities and ruthlessness towards anyone who challenged his authority. He grew up with a mother who had no real maternal instinct because she didn't learn love growing up either. She also didn't develop skills of compassion and affection. So had no way of passing on those skills to Richard and his siblings.

Richard wasn't spared when it was time for him to venture into society either. His negative experiences at home would again be echoed in his everyday experiences outside of the home. The bullying he experienced, and the loneliness he felt when his family didn't attend events, such as his communion, weighed heavily on him. Even when he committed crimes as a child, he was invisible, forgotten and overlooked.

He grew up in a time where immigrants of any nature were given the short straw, where the poor are always overlooked and disregarded. Even his own peers treated him like dirt. No child can learn how to be compassionate, caring, and respectful when the world their learning and developing mind exists in, shows no examples of that to learn from.

Societies unloving nature towards those who don't fit into its box is felt greatly by children put in positions such as Richard was. Its admiration for wealth and status created a man who was determined to have everything he was denied as a child no matter what it took to get it. Everything Richard craved; family, wealth, social status and respect could be earned through force and theft.

Society contributed to creating an, angry, detached killer through its ignorance and its cold shoulder. Richard always had the potential to be this way, genetically he was predisposed to fearlessness. He would have been able to carry out acts others just wouldn't naturally. Some people born this way go on to do great things, when this fearlessness is nurtured into acts of bravery and courage.

But for Richard this was not so, for those few who are born like this who are not loved or nurtured in early life, can go on to use this ability of fearlessness to instead commit acts of harm or destruction.

For these people, the streets offer acceptance they never found elsewhere, and crime pays. They grow up to turn against society and develop an underlying hatred for those in it who are accepted by it. They resent normality, yet also crave it, a conflicting state of mind to be in. This confliction will invite chaos and fearlessness into the person's life. They learn to hurt or be hurt. Take what they want and feel no remorse for it, after all in their mind society owes them.

It's easy to feel sorry for little Richie the boy who became the man, the boy who was unloved, unkempt, alone and afraid. For this boy you can understand his anger, his pain, his despair and his frustration at the world. He had done nothing to deserve the hand he was dealt. He just wanted to be counted for, to feel as though his life mattered to someone. But instead, he grew up learning he didn't matter, even when he committed crimes, as a young teen he wasn't noticed. Nobody cared and he knew it.

From this the man began to emerge, a man who treated people how he was treated, a man who took advantage of those in desperate situations, a man who could inflict pain as though it meant nothing, a man that would use his size and fearlessness to terrorise and kill. There is no sympathy for the man, the man who knew exactly what he was doing but chose not to stop.

For this man he will forever be remembered by those that knew him as, The Devil Himself.

Richard Leonard Kuklinski

1935 – 2006

20

Robert Dibernado
and
The Porn Racket

Robert Dibernado the Gambino Soldier

During the 1960's to the 1990's organized crime groups exploited the pornography industry and took control of it. Enabling them to expand their assets, make more money, and exert more influence over the states where they resided. These groups would use theatres, bookstores, and film companies as their legitimate business fronts. Research carried out by authorities into the network of these systems showed, that the families were working together on nationwide distribution of pornography.

Around the early 1970's the way organised crime mafia groups were operating was changing. They had begun to recruit people outside of their organisations to work as associates (these are not official mafia members; they are people the mafia do business with outside of the family). Intel collected around this time by authorities showed, "organized crime recruitment methods are changing. Although the male dominated mafia generally looked to ethnic and blood relations as a source of new members, emerging minority groups are recruiting from cell mates in prison and from street gangs" NIJ (1976)

This meant that those who were not normally involved with the mafia would be working with them directly. From store owners who aided in distribution to local criminals helping with the production of the merchandise. There was an intricate nationwide network of people from all backgrounds helping in the success of the Mafias porn racket.

A report written up by the National Institute of Justice in 1976 on organised crime stated, "Organized crime is believed to be in all aspects of the pornography industry:

literature and films of all types (i.e., hard core, soft core, art, 16mm, magazines, books), sexual devices, "service" establishments (including live sex shows), production, wholesaling and retailing, and distribution." – National Institute of Justice (1976)

Richard Kuklinski had affiliation with this racket via his job at De-Luxe Films, this was how he became associated with members of the Gambino family. When he made his deal with Roy DeMeo, to loan the money as a start-up for his bootlegging, he became tied into them. The films that he was bootlegging were ones that were owned by the film company; therefore, they were the property of DiBernado and his associates.

Richard had no choice but to get their blessing to do this. Especially as he would be doing it right under their noses, using their equipment and film. Robert DiBernado was heavily involved in the porn industry. DiBernado was born 31st May 1937, and was a soldier of the Gambino Family. Involved with various bootlegging rackets the adult industry became his niche and main earner.

Within the family, DiBernado became known as "The Pornography King", as he ran the families' pornography business, and it was later reported that he was one of the biggest pornographers in America.

Robert was never known for being involved in violence or typical mafia-business, and was mainly overseeing the pornography business, as well as engaging in extortion and labour union-rackets.

DiBernado was the largest distributor of child and 'hardcore' porn, and set up porn shops, magazines, bookstores, and other forms of pornographic material, making millions of dollars. What set DiBernado apart from the other gangsters, was that he was the only gang member who did not kill anyone; he made lucrative funds without shedding any blood.

He died 5th June 1986 at the age of 49, he was taken out by the family. His hit was arranged by John Gotti and set up by Sammy the bull, who both believed that it was time for Robert to be taken out as he was 'subversive', with him out of the way they could then take control of his assets and businesses too, profiting from the former soldier.

A meeting was arranged, and when Robert went to the meeting room, expecting a meeting to occur, it was there that he was met by his fate. In a room of associates, he was shot by Joseph "Old Man" Paruta. Robert DiBernado became Gambino history.

Below is the court testimony of Sammy 'the Bull' Gravano on the execution of Robert DiBernado

GLEESON: Did Di B come back to your office later that day?

GRAVANO: He came about five, five-thirty.

GLEESON: Did he come alone or with others?

GRAVANO: He came alone.

GLEESON: When he came, where were you?

GRAVANO: I was downstairs.

GLEESON: Is this the same location where you had the meeting to plan the murder of Paul Castellano?

GRAVANO: Yes.

GLEESON: Were you with anybody else downstairs?

GRAVANO: I was with my brother-in-law and old man Paruta.

GLEESON: Your brother-in-law being?

GRAVANO: Eddie Garafolo.

GLEESON: Was anyone upstairs when Di B came?

GRAVANO: Huck was upstairs.

GLEESON: What happened when Di B came?

GRAVANO: He told Di B that we were downstairs. Di B came in. He came downstairs. He said hello. He sat down. Then old man Paruta got up and I told him to get Di B a cup of coffee. He got up. In the cabinet there was a .380 with a silencer. He took the gun out, walked over to Di B, and shot him twice in the back of the head. Me and Eddie picked him up and put him in the back room, locked it up. We left the office.

- Testimony of Salvatore Gravano during cross examination by Gleeson at the Gotti Trial.

 **Memorandum** 4/23

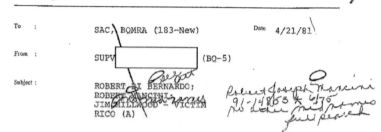

To : SAC, BQMRA (183-New)   Date 4/21/81

From : SUPV███████████ (BQ-5)

Subject : ROBERT DI BERNARDO;
ROBERT MANCINI;
JIM MILLWOOD - VICTIM
RICO (A)

    ROBERT DI BERNARDO, aka "D.B", is a soldier in
the GAMBINO Family reporting directly to PAUL CASTELLANO.
He is heavily involved in the pornography industry in the
New York area as evidenced by his recent indictment in
the MIPORN undercover operation. Enclosed are two FD-209's
detailing an extortionate loan to L.I. businessman, JIM
MILLWOOD, by DI BERNARDO and ROBERT MANCINI. It is recommended
that a RICO (A) investigation be initiated in order to
develop a prosecutable case against DI BERNARDO, MANCINI,
and their "strong arm" collectors.

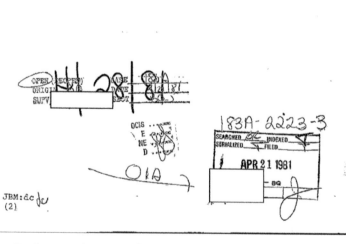

JBM:dc
(2)

Robert DiBernado FBI Memorandum

Richard Kuklinski's Police Statement

The following pages feature the police
statement of Richard Kuklinski.
The statement was taken by Jersey City
Police Department on
11th February 1980.

JERSEY CITY POLICE DEPARTMENT

TIME 1025 hours (A.M.) (X.XX) DATE Feb. 11, 1980

VICTIM-WITNESS-ID STATEMENT OF: Richard L. Kuklinski AGE 44

TAKEN AT: Homicide Squad Office, 207 - 7th Street

WITNESSED BY: Det. Sgt. [ ]

b6
b7C

I AM Detective [ ] OF THE JERSEY CITY POLICE

DEPARTMENT. DURING THIS INTERVIEW YOU ARE ASKED TO TELL ME IN YOUR OWN

WORDS WHAT TOOK PLACE ON _____ AT _____ A.M. P.M.

Q. ARE YOU WILLING TO ANSWER MY QUESTIONS AT THIS TIME? Yes.

Q. WHAT IS YOUR NAME? Richard Leonard Kuklinski

Q. WHAT IS YOUR TELEPHONE NUMBER? 384-4254

Q. WHERE DO YOU LIVE? 169 Sunset Street, Dumont, N.J. 07628

Q. WHAT IS YOUR DATE OF BIRTH? April 11, 1935

Q. WHAT IS YOUR PLACE OF BIRTH? Jersey City, N.J.

Q. WHERE DO YOU WORK? Self Employed, Wholesaler, Buy Clothes & Distribute

Q. ARE YOU MARRIED? Yes SPOUSE'S NAME? Barbara

Q. WHAT IS THE EXTENT OF YOUR EDUCATION? Graduated Grammer School

Q. CAN YOU READ AND WRITE THE ENGLISH LANGUAGE? Yes.

Q. WILL YOU NOW TELL ME IN YOUR OWN WORDS WHAT OCCURRED? Yes.
THE LAST TIME YOU SAW GEORGE W. MALLIBAND ALIVE.

A. George called me around midday Monday January 28th and asked me to

drive up to his home in Huntingdon, Pennsylvania. We were business

partners and we discussed our account over the phone and decided we

should get together. He suggested that if I had nothing to do, I

should take a ride up to his home. I'm not sure whether I called him

or he called me, I just remember the phone conversation. On TUESDAY,

January 29th I drove up to Huntingdon and I arrived George's home about

4 PM that afternonn. He wasn't home when I arrived so I went to the VFW,

about 5 minutes away at 520-22 Penn Street and waited. I had left a note

in George's door telling him where I had gone. I waited about 2 hours

before George arrived. We had a few drinks there and then went to a

local Pizzaria and dined, I don't know the name or the street it was on.

After we ate I drove George to his home and while I was there George

called the Vista-Vu Motel, on Route 22 and reserved a room for me. It's

only about ten minutes away from George's. I left George home and went

to the Motel about 10 PM to pay them for the room and get the key as

their office doesn't stay open late.

Det. Sgt. [ ]

SIGNATURE

WITNESSED BY [ ] Sgt.

Det. [ ]

PAGE 1 OF 5

b6
b7C

DD-2

CONTINUED STATEMENT OF RICHARD L. KUKLINSKI, WM AGE 44.

After picking up my key for the room I returned to George's house and picked him up and then we went back to the VFW and had a few drinks. We stayed for about 2 hours, George had received a telephone call while we were there, I don't know who the caller was, he just said he had to go somewhere. We both left the VFW at the same time, George had his own car, I didn't pick him up. I went back to the Motel. The next morning, Wednesday January 30th about 8 AM, I called George and told him I was up and we decided to meet at the TEXAS WEINERS RESTURANT in town and have breakfast. After breakfast we went back to George's house, we discussed business and watched Television. He received a couple of telephone calls while I was there, he didn't tell me who the callers were. He left the house for a few hours while I waited and slept on his couch. When he returned we went out again, had a few drinks & spent the evening together, hopping around to different places, the Moose Lodge, the Colonial Tavern, all in town. We were using George's car at this time, after we finished drinking George dropped me off at my car and we split up, I was now staying at the Best Western Motel also on Route #22, I went there and spent the night. Thursday morning, Thursday, January 31, about 8 AM I called him and told him after we had breakfast at TEXAS WEINERS, I was going to leave and go home to Dumont. He said he wanted to ride down with me and I said okay, we returned to his house where I waited while he took care of some errands. He returned and we left Huntingdon about 4 PM heading to Dumont. We stopped along the way and dined at the MIDWAY DINER on Route #78. After eating we continued and when we got on Route #17 we stopped at the HOLIDAY INN, where Route #4 & #17 meet, I think it's Paramus, George took a room there. After he got his room, I left and continued home. I went home and went to sleep, I arrived home about 10 PM that night. In the morning about 7:30 AM, I called him at the Holliday Inn and asked him what was his plans. He said he had a few errands to take care of and could he borrow my van. I said okay, I went and picked him up with my caddy and drove him back to my house in Dumont and gave him my van.

b6
b7C

TIME & DATE STATEMENT COMPLETED

Det. Sgt.

Sgt

WITNESSED BY

Det.

SIGNATURE

PAGE OF 5

CONTINUED STATEMENT OF RICHARD L. KUKLINSKI, WM, AGE 44:

It was about 8:00 AM when I picked him up at the HOLIDAY INN, I must have
called him about 7:00 AM. He left to take care of his errands and he returned a little after 10:00 AM with the van. He said he had some time to kill
and wanted to hang out for awhile so we went to my office at 428 Old Hook
Road, merson, N.J. at about 10:30 AM, he made a (few calls from my office)
and I told him I didn't want to hang around so I left him in the office
about 11:00 or 11:30 AM and I went home. Later on that day I returned to
the office, he was still there and about 2:00 or 3:00 PM he said he wanted
to go to New York. About 3:20 PM we left the office and I drove him to new
York and dropped him off at 30th Street and I think 7th Avenue, this was
about 4:00 PM. He said he wanted to make a night of it, he was going to
meet some people and go on the town. That was the last I saw or heard from
him, then [____] called me, I think it was on Sunday, February 3rd and asked
me about George and I told him I hadn't seen him since Friday when I took
him to New York. [____] said he would make a few calls to try and find
George and that was it. Ther is nothing else I can think off.

Q. - How long have you known the victim George M. Malliband?

A. - Just be between 4 and 5 years.

Q. - How long have you been business partners & what type of business?

A. - We have been doing business for the 4 or 5 years but we were only
partners for about a year. We distributed Porno Films on a freelance
basis, we didn't have a business name. We would use my business as
an address, SUNSET COMPANY, 225 Lafayette Street, New York City, tele:
212-925-3770.

Q. - What type of business is the SUNSET COMPANY & who are the owners?

A. - Clothing wholesale, I am the only owner.

Q. - When you dropped George off in New York, what arrangements were
made for his return to New Jersey?

A. - He said he would call me to pick him up when he was ready.

Det. Sgt. [____]

TIME & DATE STATEMENT COMPLETED
Det. [____]

WITNESSED BY [____]

SIGNATURE

b6
b7C

b6
b7C

PAGE 3 OF 5

CONTINUED STATEMENT OF RICHARD L. KUKLINSKI. WM. AGE 44:

Q. - Did he call you at all?

A. - No, he did not.

Q. - Did George say by name what people he was meeting in New York or
discuss the nature of his business there?

A. - No, he didn't.

Q. - Do you know if George was carrying any money or how much?

A. - He was supposed to be carrying money, but I don't know exactly how
much, he just said he was taking care of business in New York but never
mentined how much money he was carrying. He always had money.

Q. - Was George known for carrying large sums of money?

A. - There were times that George had large sums of money on him, maybe
a few thousand.

Q. - Do you know where George would get his money from?

A. - No, I don't know, you got me.

Q. - While you were in George's company, did he ever express concern about
his life or fear of being held up?

A. - He didn't say anything to me, I don't know of any enemies.

Q. - Was George known to carry a weapon of any kind?

A. - I don't think I've ever seen him with a weapon, not to my knowledge.

Q. - What happened to your van George borrowed & describe it to me?

A. - He returned it the same day I took him to New York, we left the
office in Emerson and dropped the van off at my house in Dumont on
the way to New York. The van is a Chevy, color red, 5 doors, it has
New Jersey plates XOS 39D, registered in Company's name, SUNSET.

Q. - Was he carrying anything when you picked him up at the HOLIDAY INN
Friday morning? Luggage of any type?

A. - No just a bag, brown paper bag type.

Q. - Do you own any other vehicles & describe them?

A. - I lease a car, Cadillac El Dorado, Blue & Gray from Brogan Cadillac,
Ridgewood, N.J., I also have a Cadillac, 1979 White with Blue top
registered to my mother-in-law, Genevieve Pedrin, Washington Ave,
Dumont, N.J. the plate is 500 JYY.

TIME & DATE STATEMENT COMPLETED

SIGNATURE

PAGE 4 OF 5

b6
b7C

CONTINUED STATEMENT OF RICHARD L. KUKLINSKI, WM, AGE 44:

I don't remember the plate on the leased Cadillac.

Q. - Were there any debts between you and George?

A. - He didn't owe me any money but I owed him $7,500.00 but I paid him with two checks from SUNSET COMPANY in the amounts of $4,000.00 and $3,500.00. I gave him both checks the same day, Wednesday, January 30th, at his house in Huntingdon, Pa. I asked him to hold the checks for a week before deposit. The checks were made out to George Malliband in name, First National Bank, Haworth, N.J., I dont know the account number off hand.

Q. - Were either of you insured with the other as beneficiary?

A. - No.

Q. - When did you find out that George was dead?

A. - I found out Thursday evening, February 7th, I was told by a guy named [   ] a salesman in CENTURY SALES in Pennsauken, N.J. who told b6 me he heard that George got shot and that he heard from a guy in Los b7C Angelos.

Q. - Do you know who killed George Malliband?

A. - No, I don't.

Q. - Did you kill George Malliband?

A. - No, I didn't.

Q. - Is there anything you can tell us that might help in this investigation of George's death?

A. - No, ther isn't anything I know that I haven't all ready told you.

Q. - When and whre did you live in Jersey City, N.J.

A. - From birth until I was about 18 or 19 years old, Sixteenth St., Webster Avenue, Palisade Ave and Congress St.

Q. - What is the name of the company George would buy his Porno films from?

A. - TRI-PHOTO, 21st Street, Long Island City, N.Y.

Q. - Is this a true & voluntary statement and after reading it will you sign it?

A. - Sure.

TIME & DATE STATEMENT COMPLETED 1320 FEB 1980

b6
b7C

WITNESS [   ]   SIGNATURE

PAGE 5 OF 5

Police Reports
from the
Kuklinski Investigation

The following pages feature
supplementary reports and investigation
notes from the Kuklinski investigation.
These were sourced from State archives.

FD-340 (Rev. 12-8-83)

Field File No.

OO and File No. NK49A — / 1830 —1A8

Date Received 9/23/85

From L.T.

(Name of Contributor)

JERSEY CITY P.D.

(Address of Contributor)

JERSEY CITY, N.J.

By

To Be Returned ☐ Yes   Receipt Given ☐ Yes
            ☑ No   ☑ No

            ☐ Yes   Grand Jury Material - Disseminate
            ☑ No   Only Pursuant to Rules 6(e),
                         Federal Rules of Criminal
                         Procedure

b6
b7C

Description: ☐ Original notes re interview of

① Statement (written) By
KUKLINSKI

② Supplementary Investigative
Reports re Murder of
GEORGE MALLIBUND

1 SUSPECT(S)			2 PCT/UNIT	3 SECTION CASE NUMBER	4 FILE NUMBER
	MUR		North/Homicide		#30696-80

> Victim(s) NEW ADDRESS

George W. Malliband, WM, age 42
1124 Mifflin St., Huntingdon, Pa.

5 CRIME OR SUBJECT	6 DATE OF CRIME	44 STATUS CRIME	45 STATUS CASE
Murder	Feb. 5, 1980		

5A NEW CRIME IF CHANGED	6A NJ STATUTE		
	2C:11-3	40A ADDITIONAL STOLEN PROPERTY VALUE	41A ADDITIONAL RECOVERED PROPERTY VALUE

ADDITIONAL VAL STOLEN PROPERTY	34A CURRENCY	35A JEWELRY	36A FURS	37A CLOTHING	38A AUTO	39A MISC.

LIST NAME ONLY OF PREVIOUS ACCUSED — COMPLETE INFORMATION ON NEW ACCUSED — INCLUDE ADDITIONAL PERPETRATORS — SUSPECTS — RECORD ALL DEVELOPMENTS SINCE LAST REPORT — EXPLAIN ANY CRIME CHANGE — LIST ADDITIONAL INTERVIEWS OF VICTIMS — PERSONS CONTACTED — WITNESSES — EVIDENCE — TECHNICAL SERVICES — STOLEN PROPERTY — RECOVERED PROPERTY — COURT ACTION

Accused: 46 NUMBER ACCUSED _____ 46A New accused _____ 47A ADULT _____ 48A JUVENILE _____ 49A RACE _____ 50A SEX _____ 51A DATE OF BIRTH b6

b7C

At 0930 hours, this date the belowsigned secured a statement from a

In his statement [____] relates how [____] had given him b6
a message from victim at about 4:00 or 5:00 PM, Thursday, January 31st. b7C
[____] told [____] that he had seen victim leaving home, 1124 Mifflin Street, Huntingdon, Pa., in company with Richard Kuklinski, a business partner, at about 4:00 or 4:45 PM the same day. Before leaving victim told [____] to make sure that he told [____] that he was leaving Huntingdon with Kuklinski to go to New York and that he (victim) was carrying $27,000.00 in cash. Victim wanted this information known to [____] in case anything happened to him.
b6
b7C

At about 11:30 PM, that night [____] received phone call from George Malliband who told him that he was staying at the Holiday Inn near Dumont, N.J., not far from Kuklinski's home. He gave [____] his room number & telephone. During this conversation, George told [____] that he & Kuklinski were supposed to meet with someone but he was a little concerned & hoped Kuklinski hadn't set him up. [____] said he would check back with him after he closed his bar at 2:00 AM.

Ten minutes before 3:00 AM, [____] called [____] at the Holiday b6
Inn and was assured by George that everything was alright and he promised b7C
to keep in touch. Later on that day, Friday, February 1st at about 1:00 PM
George called [____] at the bar & told him he was at Kuklinski's office.
He mentioned that the guy they were supposed to meet never showed up and again spoke of being set up. They ended their conversation discussing plans of George's birthday dinner at [____] which was scheduled for 7:00 PM, that evening. This was the last [____] heard from [____]

Sunday morning, February 3rd, [____] called Kuklinski and asked where b6
George was. Kuklinski told him he didn't know, then told him that George b7C
had left Friday afternoon to go to New York. He then said George left Friday evening and then finally he said George left at 5:30 PM. He told [____] to call him back later & hung up.

At 10:30 AM, Sunday morning [____] called Kuklinski back and asked(Cont.

52 TYPE NAME	53 BADGE		54 DATE OF REPORT
Signature [____]		PAGE 1 OF 2	[____] 18, 1980
		55 PCT/UNIT N/Homicide	56 SUPERVISOR Lt.

b6
b7C

JERSEY CITY, N.J.

SUPPLEMENTARY INVESTIGATION REPORT

POLICE DEPARTMENT

1 SUSPECT(S)		2 PCT/UNIT North/Homicide	3 SECTION CASE NUMBER	4 FILE NUMBER #30696-80

7 Victim(s) NEW ADDRESS
George W. Malliband, WM, age 42
1124 Mifflin Street,
Huntingdon, Pa.

5 CRIME OR SUBJECT Murder	6 DATE OF CRIME Feb. 5, 1980	44 STATUS CRIME	45 STATUS CASE
5A NEW CRIME IF CHANGED	6A NJ STATUTE 2C:11-3	40A ADDITIONAL STOLEN PROPERTY VALUE	41A ADDITIONAL RECOVERED PROPERTY VALUE

ADDITIONAL VAL STOLEN PROPERTY	34A CURRENCY	35A JEWELRY	36A FURS	37A CLOTHING	38A AUTO	39A MISC.

LIST NAME ONLY OF PREVIOUS ACCUSED — COMPLETE INFORMATION ON NEW ACCUSED — INCLUDE ADDITIONAL PERPETRATORS — SUSPECTS — RECORD ALL DEVELOPMENTS SINCE LAST REPORT — EXPLAIN ANY CRIME CHANGE — LIST ADDITIONAL INTERVIEWS OF VICTIMS — PERSONS CONTACTED — WITNESSES — EVIDENCE — TECHNICAL SERVICES — STOLEN PROPERTY — RECOVERED PROPERTY — COURT ACTION

Accused: 46 NUMBER ACCUSED _____ 46A New accused _____ 47A ADULT _____ 48A JUVENILE _____ 49A RACE _____ 50A SEX _____ 51A DATE OF BIRTH

(Cont.)

him had he heard from George and was told "no". [   ] then asked him b6
how did George get to New York and what had happened to the money George b7C
was carrying. Kuklinski said this time, that he had driven George to New
York on Friday and dropped him off somewhere on 30th Street. As for the
money, Kuklinski stated that George took it with him. In regards to George
returning home for the birthday dinner, Kuklinski told [   ] George had
changed his plans. Kuklinski said he had nothing else to offer about George
disappearance and the conversation ended.   b6
                                                                            b7C

Sunday, February 3rd, [   ] called Pennsylvania State Police, Huntingdon Barracks and reported to Trooper [   ] that [   ] George Malliband was missing.

Monday, February 4th, a [   ] of Yonkers, N.Y., tele: b6
[   ] called [   ] and informed him that George had paid him a b7C
visit, at his home in Yonkers, February 1st at 9:00 AM. He also said that
he had a telephone conversation with George later that same day about 3:30
PM while George was in Kuklinski's office in Dumont, N.J., adding that he
called George using a Dumont, N.J. number. [   ] told [   ] that he felt
victim was worried about something but did not elaborate. He did not hear
from or see George again.

In [   ] statement he says that he does not know why [   ]
[   ] was carrying so much money and assumes the money was to buy porno b6
films. That was the only time he would carry large sums of money to his b7C
knowledge. He would sometimes carry the money in a paper bag or his pocket.

In regards to threats or outstanding debts [   ] said that he does b6
not know of anyone that might of threatened [   ] life. He does b7C
know that Kuklinski owed [   ] $35,000.00 as a result of business
transaction with porno films. To his knowledge the debt was never cleared
and Kuklinski had been stalling [   ] about payment.

In conclusion, [   ] stated that this was the only information he could offer at this time.

Investigation to Continue....

52 TYPE NAME Det. [ ]	54 BADGE	53 PAGE 2 OF 2	54 DATE OF REPORT [ ] 1980	b6
Signature [ ]		55 PCT/UNIT N/Homicide	56 SUPERVISOR Lt. [ ]	b7C

RECORD ROOM COPY

1 SUSPECT(S)		2 PCT/UNIT	3 SECTION CASE NUMBER	4 FILE NUMBER
		NO. HOM. SQ		30696

		7 Victim(s) NEW ADDRESS		DOB 2/1/38
5 CRIME OR SUBJECT	6 DATE OF CRIME	GEORGE WILLIAM MALLIBAND JR.		
MURDER.	2/5/80	1124 MIFFLIN ST. HUNTINGDON PA.		

5A NEW CRIME IF CHANGED	6A NJ STATUTE	44 STATUS CRIME		45 STATUS CASE	
	2C: 11-3				
		40A ADDITIONAL STOLEN PROPERTY VALUE		41A ADDITIONAL RECOVERED PROPERTY VALUE	

ADDITIONAL VAL STOLEN PROPERTY	34A CURRENCY	35A JEWELRY	36A FURS	37A CLOTHING	38A AUTO	39A MISC.

LIST NAME ONLY OF PREVIOUS ACCUSED — COMPLETE INFORMATION ON NEW ACCUSED — INCLUDE ADDITIONAL PERPETRATORS — SUSPECTS — RECORD ALL DEVELOPMENTS SINCE LAST REPORT — EXPLAIN ANY CRIME CHANGE — LIST ADDITIONAL INTERVIEWS OF VICTIMS — PERSONS CONTACTED — WITNESSES — EVIDENCE — TECHNICAL SERVICES — STOLEN PROPERTY — RECOVERED PROPERTY — COURT ACTION

Accused: 46 NUMBER ACCUSED _____ 46A New accused _____ 47A ADULT _____ 48A JUVENILE _____ 49A RACE _____ 50A SEX _____ 51A DATE OF BIRTH

At 0930 Hours this date 2/7/80 the U/S Phoned the "BROGAN CADILLAC CO."
Paterson Office, located at 505 Ellison Street Paterson N.J. Phone
742 8400 in Re: to a 1979 Cadillac N.J. Reg. 813 KPY two door, Color   b6
Blue and Grey listed to the above company.   b7C

Spoke to a [   ] who checked Company records and gave the following information:

That this vehicle was leased on May 25th, 1979 to "Sunset Co". 169 Sunset
Drive Dumont N.J. , Phone # 385 5548. A Richard Kuklinski who listed
himself as Vice President of Sunset Co. signed a 36 month lease for this
automobile, and it is still in his possession.

Mr. Kuklinski gave the following N.J. Dr. Lic Number K 9 188 65 57304352.
The U/S also contacted Sgt [   ] of the J.C. Auto Squad and requested
an Alphabetical Check of the Above Kuklinski.   b6

Sgt. [   ] gave the following information: Kuklinski has no Vehicles b7C
registered to him, also has the same Dr. Lic. listed above. He gave
the place of employment as the "Sunset Co. 125 Lafayette S. N.Y.C.
Check with the N.Y.C. Phone Directory shows no Phone listed at this address.
Check with N.Y. City Phone information shows no listing or Phone for this
Sunset Co at 125 Lafayette St. N.Y.C.

b6
b7C

Sgt. [   ]

52 TYPE NAME		53		54 DATE OF REPORT
		PAGE 1 OF 1 PAGES		2/7/80
Signature Sgt		55 PCT/UNIT Hom. Sq.	56 SUPERVISOR	

RECORD ROOM COPY

JERSEY CITY, N.J.

SUPPLEMENTARY
INVESTIGATION REPORT

POLICE DEPARTMENT

1 SUSPECT(S)		2 PCT/UNIT	3 SECTION CASE NUMBER	4 FILE NUMBER
		North-HOM		30696

		7 Victim(s) NEW ADDRESS
5 CRIME OR SUBJECT	6 DATE OF CRIME	George Malliband Jr. W M age 42
Murder	2-5-80	1124 Mifflin St.
		Huntingdon, Pa.

5A NEW CRIME IF CHANGED	6A NJ STATUTE	44 STATUS CRIME	45 STATUS CASE
	2 C 11-3	Invest.	Open

		40A ADDITIONAL STOLEN PROPERTY VALUE	41A ADDITIONAL RECOVERED PROPERTY VALUE

ADDITIONAL VAL STOLEN PROPERTY	34A CURRENCY	35A JEWELRY	36A FURS	37A CLOTHING	38A AUTO	39A MISC.

LIST NAME ONLY OF PREVIOUS ACCUSED — COMPLETE INFORMATION ON NEW ACCUSED — INCLUDE ADDITIONAL PERPETRATORS — SUSPECTS — RECORD ALL DEVELOPMENTS SINCE LAST REPORT — EXPLAIN ANY CRIME CHANGE — LIST ADDITIONAL INTERVIEWS OF VICTIMS — PERSONS CONTACTED — WITNESSES — EVIDENCE — TECHNICAL SERVICES — STOLEN PROPERTY — RECOVERED PROPERTY — COURT ACTION

Accused: 46 NUMBER ACCUSED _____ 46A New accused _____ 47A ADULT _____ 48A JUVENILE _____ 49A RACE   50A SEX   51A DATE OF BIRTH

At 11:00 hours this date, the undersigned by phone, did interview the

                        relative to any information he   b6
could provide about the victim.   stated that on Jan. 31, 1980   b7C
between 2 P. M. and 3 P. M.
saw the victim in front of his home (1124 Mifflin St. Huntington, PA.)
with Richard Kuklinski, W M age 45, res. 169 Sunset Drive, Dumont, N. J.
and they were in a Blue/Gray Cadillac, N. J. 813 and the victim stated that
they were going to New Jersey and that he had $27000.00 in cash on him and
wanted   to make sure and tell
     about this in case anything happened to him.

    Following is a sequence of events in relation to the victim:
1-31-80 (11:30 PM and 12 Mid.) Victim phoned   b6
      from the Holiday Inn, Paramus, N. J. Room #220 (843-5400) and stated b7C
      that he was worried about something but he would not elaborate.

2-1-80 (3 AM)   called the victim at the Holiday Inn and the   b6
      victim stated that everything was alright.   b7C

2-1-80 (1 PM) Victim called   and stated that he b6
      felt that something was going wrong but would not elaborate.   b7C
          felt that the call was being made from the office of
      Richard Kuklinski. (Sunset Co. 169 Sunset Dr. Dumont, N. J. although
      he could not be sure of this.(THIS IS THE LAST TIME THAT
      EVER HEARD FROM   GEORGE MALLIBAND JR.)

      Victim was supposed to return home for his birthday Feb. 1, 1980

2-2-80 (11 PM)   called Richard Kuklinski at his business   b6
      number 201-385-5548 and got the answering service where he left a mess b7C
      to have Richard Kuklinski call him.

2-3-80 (8:30 AM)   called George Kuklinski and asked him where b6
      George was. Richard kuklinski stated that George on 2-2-80 WENT to   b7C
      New York City to get LAID and get a MASSAGE.

                                                  b6
                                                  b7C

52 TYPE NAME	53 BADGE	53 PAGE 1 2	54 DATE OF REPORT Feb. 6, 1980
Signature Lt.		55 PCT/UNIT N-HOM	56 Lt.

RECORD ROOM COPY

1 SUSPECT(S)				2 PCT/UNIT North-HOM	3 SECTION CASE NUMBER	4 FILE NUMBER .30696

				7 Victim(s) NEW ADDRESS George Malliband Jr. 1124 Mifflin St. Huntingdon, PA.		

5 CRIME OR SUBJECT Murder	6 DATE OF CRIME 2-5-80			44 STATUS CRIME		45 STATUS CASE
5A NEW CRIME IF CHANGED	6A NJ STATUTE 2 C 11-3			40A ADDITIONAL STOLEN PROPERTY VALUE		41A ADDITIONAL RECOVERED PROPERTY VALUE

ADDITIONAL VAL STOLEN PROPERTY	34A CURRENCY	35A JEWELRY	36A FURS	37A CLOTHING	38A AUTO	39A MISC.

LIST NAME ONLY OF PREVIOUS ACCUSED – COMPLETE INFORMATION ON NEW ACCUSED – INCLUDE ADDITIONAL PERPETRATORS – SUSPECTS – RECORD ALL DEVELOPMENTS SINCE LAST REPORT – EXPLAIN ANY CRIME CHANGE – LIST ADDITIONAL INTERVIEWS OF VICTIMS – PERSONS CONTACTED – WITNESSES – EVIDENCE – TECHNICAL SERVICES – STOLEN PROPERTY – RECOVERED PROPERTY – COURT ACTION

Accused: 46 NUMBER ACCUSED	46A New accused	47A ADULT	48A JUVENILE	49A RACE	50A SEX	51A DATE OF BIRTH

2-3-80 (5 PM) [   ] called Richard Kuklinski as to the whereabouts b6
of George and R. Kuklinski stated that he TOOK him to New York City   b7C
on 2-2-80 and dropped him off at 30 St. N. Y. C. where he was going
to get LAID ETC.

    Investigation of the movements of the victim while intthis area indicated
that he checked into the Holiday Inn, Paramus, N. J. Room #220 on 1-31-80
at 11:56 PM paid $34.65 for the room (1 Person) and evidently checked out
before 12 Noon on 2-1-80 Subject gave his right name and address at the
Holiday Inn.

    The vehicle in question, N. J. 813-KPY checks out to the Brogan Auto
Leasing Co. 100 South Broad St. Ridgewood, N. J. a 1979 Cadillac, color
Blue Gray, 2 Door, expired May 1980. Check with this company revealed that
this vehicle was rented to Richard Kuklinski on May 25, 1979 on a 36 month
lease and the vehicle is still in possession of Richard Kuklinski.

    Investigation is continuing.

b6
b7C

52 TYPE NAME Lt. Signature	58 BADGE	53 PAGE 2	55 PCT/UNIT N-HOM	56 Lt.	54 DATE OF REPORT Feb. 6, 1980

RECORD ROOM COPY

SUPPLEMENTARY
INVESTIGATION REPORT

POLICE DEPARTMENT

1 SUSPECT(S)		2 PCT/UNIT No. Hom. Sq.	3 SECTION CASE NUMBER	4 FILE NUMBER 3 0 6 9 6

7 Victim(s) NEW ADDRESS
George William Malliband JR.
1124 Mifflin St. Huntingdon Pa.

5 CRIME OR SUBJECT Murder	6 DATE OF CRIME PC: 11-2/5/80 3		
5A NEW CRIME IF CHANGED	6A NJ STATUTE PC: 11-1	44 STATUS CRIME	45 STATUS CASE
		46A ADDITIONAL STOLEN PROPERTY VALUE	41A ADDITIONAL RECOVERED PROPERTY VALUE

ADDITIONAL VAL STOLEN PROPERTY	34A CURRENCY	35A JEWELRY	36A FURS	37A CLOTHING	38A AUTO	39A MISC.

LIST NAME ONLY OF PREVIOUS ACCUSED – COMPLETE INFORMATION ON NEW ACCUSED – INCLUDE ADDITIONAL PERPETRATORS – SUSPECTS – RECORD ALL DEVELOPMENTS SINCE LAST REPORT – EXPLAIN ANY CRIME CHANGE – LIST ADDITIONAL INTERVIEWS OF VICTIMS – PERSONS CONTACTED – WITNESSES – EVIDENCE – TECHNICAL SERVICES – STOLEN PROPERTY – RECOVERED PROPERTY – COURT ACTION

Accused: 46 NUMBER ACCUSED _____ 46A New accused _____ 47A ADULT _____ 48A JUVENILE _____ 49A RACE _____ 50A SEX _____ 51A DATE OF BIRTH

At 1400 Hours 2/7/80 the U/S phoned the home of Richard Kuklinski
DOB 4/11/35, Res. 169 Sunset Drive Dumont N.J. in an attempt to made an
appointment with him in Re: to the above incident. Spoke to a female who
stated that she was Barbara Kuklinsk the wife of Richard Kuklinski, who
stated that Richard Kuklinski was not at home. She further stated that he
left on a trip to the "South" this A.M. but she did not know his destination.
She expects to hear from him by phone this evening (2/7/80).
I requested Mrs Kuklinski that if her husband contacts her , to have him
contact the J.C. Police on 2/8/80 at 547-5476 J.C. Homicide Office
Phone Number.
I told Mrs. Kuklinski that we wished to talk to her husband in Re: to a
Police incident but did not tell her the nature of this investigation.

Sgt.

b6
b7C

52 TYPE NAME	53 PAGE 1 OF 1	54 DATE OF REPORT
Signature	55 PCT/UNIT Hom Sq.	56 SUPERVISOR APP.

JERSEY CITY, N.J.

SUPPLEMENTARY
INVESTIGATION REPORT

POLICE DEPARTMENT

1 SUSPECT(S)			2 PCT/UNIT NO. HOM SQ.	3 SECTION CASE NUMBER	4 FILE NUMBER 3 0 6 9 6
			7 Victim(s) NEW ADDRESS George William Malliband JR. 1124 Mifflin St. Huntingdon PA.		DOB 2/1/38
5 CRIME OR SUBJECT MURDER		6 DATE OF CRIME ?/5/80			
5A NEW CRIME IF CHANGED		6A NJ STATUTE 2C: 11-3	44 STATUS CRIME	45 STATUS CASE	
			40A ADDITIONAL STOLEN PROPERTY VALUE	41A ADDITIONAL RECOVERED PROPERTY VALUE	

ADDITIONAL VAL STOLEN PROPERTY	34A CURRENCY	35A JEWELRY	36A FURS	37A CLOTHING	38A AUTO	39A MISC.

LIST NAME ONLY OF PREVIOUS ACCUSED — COMPLETE INFORMATION ON NEW ACCUSED — INCLUDE ADDITIONAL PERPETRATORS — SUSPECTS — RECORD ALL DEVELOPMENTS SINCE LAST REPORT — EXPLAIN ANY CRIME CHANGE — LIST ADDITIONAL INTERVIEWS OF VICTIMS — PERSONS CONTACTED — WITNESSES — EVIDENCE — TECHNICAL SERVICES — STOLEN PROPERTY — RECOVERED PROPERTY — COURT ACTION

Accused: 46 NUMBER ACCUSED _____ 46A New accused _____ 47A ADULT _____ 48A JUVENILE _____ 49A RACE   50A SEX   51A DATE OF BIRTH

On 2/6/80 the U/S conducted a background Check in Re: to a Richard Kuklinski.
Check with J.C. BCI shows a Richard Kuklinski, DOB 4/11/35 , listed as
living at 39 Newkirk St. J.C. in 1958. Has arrest Record in J.C. for AA&B
Receiving Stolen Prop. and Fugative from Armed Forced. Has J.C. BCI
Number of 18620. Hudson County BCI # 46367. Physical Description
6' 4" , 230 lbs, Brown Hair and Brown Eyes. FBI # 8565D, SP#. 571114
Last arrested in Hudson County for Violation of City Ord. in Union City N.J.
on 10/10/66. He gave his address at that time as 617 57th St. West New York.

He now resides at 169 Sunset Drive Dumont N.J. Phone 385 0481

Check with the Bergen County Sheriff's Office in Re: to Richard Kuklinski
th Negative results, no record in Bergen County.

Last I.D. Picture of Kuklinski in the J.C. BCI was in 1958.
A Union City BCI Picture of Kuklinski was obtained this date from the
Union City P.D.

Sgt.			
52 TYPE NAME	53 PAGE 1 OF 1	54 DATE OF REPORT 0/0/80	b6 b7C
Signature	55 PCT/UNIT Hom Sq.	56 SUPERVISOR	

RECORD ROOM COPY

	SUPPLEMENTARY INVESTIGATION REPORT		POLICE DEPARTMENT

1 SUSPECT(S)	2 PCT/UNIT No. Homicide	3 SECTION CASE NUMBER	4 FILE NUMBER 30696

Victim(s) NEW ADDRESS
George W. Malliband Jr. Age 42
1124 Mifflin St. Huntingdon PA.

5 CRIME OR SUBJECT Murder	6 DATE OF CRIME 2/5/80		
5A NEW CRIME IF CHANGED	6A NJ STATUTE PC:11-3	44 STATUS CRIME	45 STATUS CASE
		40A ADDITIONAL STOLEN PROPERTY VALUE	41A ADDITIONAL RECOVERED PROPERTY VALUE

ADDITIONAL VAL STOLEN PROPERTY	34A CURRENCY	35A JEWELRY	36A FURS	37A CLOTHING	38A AUTO	39A MISC.

LIST NAME ONLY OF PREVIOUS ACCUSED – COMPLETE INFORMATION ON NEW ACCUSED – INCLUDE ADDITIONAL PERPETRATORS – SUSPECTS – RECORD ALL DEVELOPMENTS SINCE LAST REPORT – EXPLAIN ANY CRIME CHANGE – LIST ADDITIONAL INTERVIEWS OF VICTIMS – PERSONS CONTACTED – WITNESSES – EVIDENCE – TECHNICAL SERVICES – STOLEN PROPERTY – RECOVERED PROPERTY – COURT ACTION

Accused: 46 NUMBER ACCUSED _____ 46A New accused _____ 47A ADULT _____ 48A JUVENILE _____ 49A RACE _____ 50A SEX _____ 53A DATE OF BIRTH

On 2/18/80 [ ] visited the Homicide office where
he was interviewed and gave a statement to Det. [ ] which was
covered in a previous report. During this interview [ ] did
turn over to the U/S the following items:
A Photo Copy of a Check issued by the " Barclays Bank International Limited"
Tortola B. V. I. Branch. Dated 12/17/79, # 0230773, Pay to the Order of
[ ] for the Sum of $ 28,514.01 and endorsed on the Rear of Check
by [ ] then " Pay to the Order of '
[ ] and G. Malliband.
[ ] stated that [ ] George Malliband accompanied by a
male, possibly [ ] cashed the above check in "The First
National Bank " of Mapleton Huntingdon Pa. in the Smithfield Office of this
bank where the victim has his Account. This Check was Cashed on 1/30/80.
[ ] stated that [ ] George received $20,000 from this
check and [ ] received the remainder, $ 8,514.01. [ ] did not
know anything else about this transaction or about [ ]
The U/S also received from [ ] a Check # 700, Dated 1/29/80
drawn on the Account of Sunset Company Box 261, Phone 210 385 5548 Dumont
N.J. 07628, Signed by Richard Kuklinski , " First National State Bank Haworth
N.J.; Pay to the Order of George Malliband, the Sum of $ 4000.00. Endorsed
on the back George Malliband, and Cashed by George Malliband in the First
National Bank of Mapleton, Huntingdon Pa.
[ ] had spoke to the Teller of the First National Bank in
Huntingdon, and verified that [ ] George Malliband did Cash the
above two Checks.

52 TYPE NAME Sgt.	59 BADGE	53 PAGE 1 OF 3	54 DATE OF REPORT 2/20/80
Signature SGT.		55 PCT/UNIT Hom. Sq.	56 SUPERVISOR

SPECIFIC OFFENSE		SECTION CASE NO.	FILE NO
MURDER			3 0 6 9 6

STATUTE OR ORDINANCE (R.S., N.J.S., REV. OR O.)	LOCATION OF OFFENSE	DATE OF OCCURENCE
2C:11-3	# # Hope Street J.C.	2/5/80

[   ] gave the U/S the following list of Credit Cards in the name [b6 b7C]

of George Malliband Jr. which was in the victim's wallet and not recovered

during the search of the victim's body:

Mobile Credit Card   # 880 370 512 11

Texico   "   "   # 53 864 1020 2 W

Gulf   "   "   # 22029 18559 0382 J

Visa   "   "   # 4261 560 508 859

American Ex.   "   # 3721 3229000 41004

A "STOP" was put on the above Credit Cards by [   ] [b6 b7C]

Also received by the U/S from [   ] phone bills from George Malliband

Bell of Pennsylvania . Account. for victim's Phone # 814 643 6096. These

for the Months of Aug., Sept., Oct., and Nov. of 1979. [   ]

will forward the Telephone bills of victim for Dec. and Jan. 1980 when he

receives them.

All above items marked by the U/S "W M 2/18/80 G M" and will be put into

the J.C. Property Room, as evidence.

At 1000 Hours 2/20/80 the U/S in company with Lt. [   ] visited [b6 b7C]

the First National Bank, Haworth where [   ] gave us two

Photo Copies of Checks, # 700 , drawn on the account of Sunset Company

(Robert Kuklinski) Dated 1/29/80, Pay to the Order of George Malliband the

Sum of $4000.00, this check the same as previously mentioned in this report.

Also received from [   ] two Photo Copies of Check # 699 Drawn on the

account of Sunset Company (Richard Kuklinski) First National Bank of Haworth

Dated 1/29/80, Pay to the Order of George Malliband the sum of $3500.00.

This check also endorsed on the back by George Malliband. This check also

cashed by the victim prior to leaving Penn. on Thursday Jan 31st. 1980.

These will be marked by the U/S and placed into evidence.

AMENDED PROPERTY VALUATION	A. CURRENCY	B. JEWELRY	C. FURS	D. CLOTHING	E. LOCAL AUTO	F. MISCELLANEOUS	G. TOTALS

RANK	SIGNATURE OF OFFICER SUBMITTING REPORT	PCT/UNIT	BADGE NUMBER
Sgt.		Hom. Sq.	b6

STATUS OF C	STATUS OF CASE	
☐ UNFOUNDED ☐ CLEARED BY ARREST ☒ NOT CLEARED ☐ EXCEPTIONALLY CLEARED	☐ PENDING ACTIVE ☐ PENDING INACTIVE ☐ CLOSED	b7C

CLEARED BY ARREST OF	CLASSIFICATION:	RECLASSIFICATION:
☐ JUV. ☐ ADULT ☐ JUV. & ☐ NARCOTIC OFFENDER		

DATE	TALLIED BY:	INDEXED BY:
2/20/80		

SUPERVISOR APPROVING	FILED BY	PAGE NUMBER: 2	NO. OF PAGES: 3

RECORD ROOM COPY

SPECIFIC OFFENSE Murder		SECTION CASE NO.	FILE NO 30696
STATUTE OR ORDINANCE (R.S., N.J.S., REV. OR O.) 2C:11-3	LOCATION OF OFFENSE # 3 Hope St. J.C		DATE OF OCCURENCE 2/5/80

Lt. [   ] and the U/S also visited the Office of "Sunset Com- b6
pany 428 B Old Hook Road Emerson N.J. Telephone # 967 5732, but found no b7C
one at that location as the Office was closed.

Spoke to a [   ] of "Stevens Association" at the next door locati b6
and he stated that he is in his office Mon. to Fri. from 0900 Hours to b7C
1630 Hours, and comes in on Saturdays at 1000 Hours. He stated that he
did not see or hear anything unusual on 2/1/80. He knows Richard Kuklinski
but does not recall seeing him with any body fitting the description of the
victim, George Malliband.

Also spoke to Richard Kuklinski's landlord, one [   ] of " T & G" b6
Associates" 436 Old Hook Road Emerson N.J. who stated that he stays in b7C
his Office from till five or six P.M., and often comes in on Saturday
mornings. He did not see or hear anything unusual on 2/1/80 or the morning
of 2/3/80.

Also passed by the home of Richard Kuklinski 169 Sunset Street Dumont N.J.
this a one family, two story structure with driveway. Parked in driveway b6
was a Maroon Van , N.J. Reg. XOS 39 D that Richard Kuklinski during b7C
interview on 2/11/80 said belong to him. Check with the Computor shows
this plate issued to a Red Chev., 1974 Pick Up, and owned by a
[   ]

This Van has a passenger door on right side also a Sliding door on the right
side, and two door at the rear; also a door on left side used by driver.
There is partition between the front seat of van and the rear of van that
makes it impossible to make a visual observation from the front seat to the
rear of van. No glass in this van other than the Windshield.

AMENDED PROPERTY VALUATION	A. CURRENCY	B. JEWELRY	C. FURS	D. CLOTHING	E. LOCAL AUTO	F. MISCELLANEOUS	G. TOTALS

RANK Sgt.			PCT/UNIT Hom. Sq.		BADGE NUMBER
STATUS OF OFF ☐ UNFOUNDE		STATUS OF CASE ☒ PENDING ACTIVE ☐ PENDING INACTIVE ☐ CLOSED			b6 b7C
CLEARED BY ARREST OF: ☐ JUV. ☐ ADULT ☐ JUV. & ADULT ☐ NARCOTIC OFFENDER		CLASSIFICATION:	RECLASSIFICATION:		
[signature] SUPERVISOR	DATE 2/2-/80	TALLIED BY:	INDEXED BY:		
		FILED BY	PAGE NUMBER 3	NO. OF PAGES: 3

1 SUSPECT(S)		2 PCT/UNIT	3 SECTION CASE NUMBER	4 FILE NUMBER
		North-HOM.		30696

7 Victim(s) NEW ADDRESS
George Malliband Jr. W M Age 42
1124 Mifflin St.
Huntingdon, Pa.

5 CRIME OR SUBJECT	6 DATE OF CRIME		
Murder	2-5-80		

5A NEW CRIME IF CHANGED	6A NJ STATUTE	44 STATUS CRIME	45 STATUS CASE
	2 C 11-3	Investigation	Open
		40A ADDITIONAL STOLEN PROPERTY VALUE	41A ADDITIONAL RECOVERED PROPERTY VALUE

ADDITIONAL VAL STOLEN PROPERTY	34A CURRENCY	35A JEWELRY	36A FURS	37A CLOTHING	38A AUTO	39A MISC.

LIST NAME ONLY OF PREVIOUS ACCUSED — COMPLETE INFORMATION ON NEW ACCUSED — INCLUDE ADDITIONAL PERPETRATORS — SUSPECTS — RECORD ALL DEVELOPMENTS SINCE LAST REPORT — EXPLAIN ANY CRIME CHANGE — LIST ADDITIONAL INTERVIEWS OF VICTIMS — PERSONS CONTACTED — WITNESSES — EVIDENCE — TECHNICAL SERVICES — STOLEN PROPERTY — RECOVERED PROPERTY — COURT ACTION

Accused: 46 NUMBER ACCUSED _____ 46A New accused _____ 47A ADULT _____ 48A JUVENILE _____ 49A RACE   50A SEX   51A DATE OF BIRTH

At 14:00 hours this date, the undersigned responded to the De Luxe Graphic Arts Co. 225 Lafayette St. New York City, N. Y. Room #1005 to interview ▓▓▓▓▓▓▓▓▓▓▓▓▓▓▓▓▓▓▓▓▓ as to any information he might have relative to the above subject. ▓▓▓▓▓▓ stated that at NO time did he ever do any type of business with the victim, George Malliband and had only seen him three or four times. Each time he had seen the victim he was in company with RICHARD KUKLINSKI, W. M. AGE 45 RES. 169 SUNSET ST. DUMONT, NEW JERSEY in the area of 225 Lafayette St. N. Y. C. and the last time he saw him was about two months ago and at that time, he, Richard Kuklinski and the victim had lunch at the Bok Hop Chinese Rest. located at 224 Lafayette St. N. Y. C.

     b6
     b7C

The undersigned also on this date did visit the office of Richard Kuklinski, 225 Lafayette St. N. Y. C. Room 1004 but there was no response. Regarding this office, from information received from ▓▓▓▓▓▓▓▓ Richard Kuklinski maintained this office so as to be in proximity to a Film Lab located at 75 Spring St. N. Y. C. which has since moved to somewhere in Queens, New York. Richard Kuklinski's office uses the trade name of SUNSET COMPANY, 225 Lafayette St. N. Y. C. Room # 1004.

     b6
     b7C

Investigation is continuing.

     b6
     b7C

52 TYPE NAME	58 BADGE	53 PAGE 1 OF	54 DATE OF REPORT
Signature Lt. Sgt.			5, 1980.
		55 PCT/UNIT North-Hom.	56 SUPERVISOR Lt.

1 SUSPECT(S)			2 PCT/UNIT	3 SECTION CASE NUMBER	4 FILE NUMBER
			North/Homicide		#30696-80

7 Victim(s) NEW ADDRESS

5 CRIME OR SUBJECT	6 DATE OF CRIME	7 Victim(s)
Murder	Feb. 5, 1980	George W. Malliband, WM, age 42
		1124 Mifflin Street, Huntingdon, Pa.

5A NEW CRIME IF CHANGED	6A NJ STATUTE	44 STATUS CRIME	45 STATUS CASE
	2C:11-3		

	40A ADDITIONAL STOLEN PROPERTY VALUE	41A ADDITIONAL RECOVERED PROPERTY VALUE

ADDITIONAL VAL STOLEN PROPERTY	34A CURRENCY	35A JEWELRY	36A FURS	37A CLOTHING	38A AUTO	39A MISC.

LIST NAME ONLY OF PREVIOUS ACCUSED – COMPLETE INFORMATION ON NEW ACCUSED – INCLUDE ADDITIONAL PERPETRATORS – SUSPECTS – RECORD ALL DEVELOPMENTS SINCE LAST REPORT – EXPLAIN ANY CRIME CHANGE – LIST ADDITIONAL INTERVIEWS OF VICTIMS – PERSONS CONTACTED – WITNESSES – EVIDENCE – TECHNICAL SERVICES – STOLEN PROPERTY – RECOVERED PROPERTY – COURT ACTION

Accused: 46 NUMBER ACCUSED ____ 46A New accused ____ 47A ADULT ____ 48A JUVENILE ____ 49A RACE ____ 50A SEX ____ 51A DATE OF BIRTH

At 1015 hours, this date Mr. Richard L. KUKLINSKI, WM, age 44, res: b6
169 Sunset Street, Dumont, N.J., tele: 384-4254, arrived this office for b7C
scheduled interview and statement. It was learned thru investigation that
KUKLINSKI was observed driving victim away from his home in Huntingdon on
January 31, 1980, early afternoon. Before leaving, victim informed his
_____ that he was carrying $27,000.00 in
cash and was heading to New Jersey in KUKLINSKI's 1979 Cadillac, El Dorado,
Blue/Gray, N.J. Reg. 813 KPY, leased from Brogan Cadillac, Ridgewood, N.J.

The following are series of events as told by KUKLINSKI up to the last
time he saw George Malliband alive:

Mr KUKLINSKI stated that he and victim have been business partners for
about a year, dealing in Pornographic Film Distribution. Tuesday, January
29th, he drove up to victim's home in Huntingdon so that they could discuss their accounts and socialize. He remained in Huntingdon until Thursday, January 31st when he decided to return Home to Dumont, N.J. Victim
asked if he could go along and they both left Huntingdon about 4:00 PM
that day heading for Dumont, N.J.

When they reached New Jersey Route #17 near Route #4, victim checked
in at the HOLIDAY INN, Paramus, N.J. KUKLINSKI continued home to Dumont.
The following day Friday, February 1st, about 7:00 AM he called victim at
the HOLIDAY INN & asked him what his plans were. Victim asked him for the
use of his Van as he had some errands to run. KUKLINSKI drove to the HOLI-
DAY INN, arrived around 8:00 AM, brought victim back to Dumont & loaned
him the Van, color red with N.J. Reg. XOS 39D. Victim returned with van
10:00 AM. They then went to KUKLINSKI's office, 428 Old Hook Road, Emerson,
N.J. (SUNSET CO.) at 10:30 AM where victim stayed until after 3:00 PM.

Victim told KUKLINSKI that he wanted to go to New York City to meet
some people, go on the town & make a night of it. At about 3:20 PM they
left Emerson, N.J. & headed to New York where he dropped victim off in
the vicinity of 30th Street & 7th Avenue approximately 4:00 PM.

KUKLINSKI further stated that victim was to call him when he was ready
to return to New Jersey, but he never heard from him again.

52 TYPE NAME	53 BADGE	53		54 DATE OF REPORT
Signature _ Det. _		PAGE 1 OF 2		80
		55 PCT/UNIT	56 SUPERVISOR	b6
		N/Homicide	Lt.	b7C

SUPPLEMENTARY
INVESTIGATION REPORT

POLICE DEPARTMENT

1 SUSPECT(S)		2 PCT/UNIT	3 SECTION CASE NUMBER	4 FILE NUMBER
		North/Homicide		#30696-80

7 Victim(s) NEW ADDRESS

George W. Malliband, WM, age 42
1124 Mifflin St., Huntingdon, Pa.

5 CRIME OR SUBJECT	6 DATE OF CRIME	44 STATUS CRIME	45 STATUS CASE
Murder	Feb. 5, 1980		
5A NEW CRIME IF CHANGED	6A NJ STATUTE	40A ADDITIONAL STOLEN PROPERTY VALUE	41A ADDITIONAL RECOVERED PROPERTY VALUE
	2C:11-3		

ADDITIONAL VAL STOLEN PROPERTY	34A CURRENCY	35A JEWELRY	36A FURS	37A CLOTHING	38A AUTO	39A MISC.

LIST NAME ONLY OF PREVIOUS ACCUSED — COMPLETE INFORMATION ON NEW ACCUSED — INCLUDE ADDITIONAL PERPETRATORS — SUSPECTS — RECORD ALL DEVELOPMENTS SINCE LAST REPORT — EXPLAIN ANY CRIME CHANGE — LIST ADDITIONAL INTERVIEWS OF VICTIMS — PERSONS CONTACTED — WITNESSES — EVIDENCE — TECHNICAL SERVICES — STOLEN PROPERTY — RECOVERED PROPERTY — COURT ACTION

Accused: 46 NUMBER ACCUSED _____ 46A New accused _____ 47A ADULT _____ 48A JUVENILE _____ 49A RACE   50A SEX   51A DATE OF BIRTH

Also in the statement KUKLINSKI mentions that he has known victim for approximately 4 or 5 years although theyv'e only been partners for one. The business they shared was Pornographic Film Distribution on a freelance basis, using KUKLINSKI's self-owned business address, SUNSET COMPANY, 225 Lafayette St., New York City, tele: 212-925-3770 with another office in Emerson, N.J. Sunset Company is for Clothing Wholesale. Porno Films would be purchased from TRI-PHOTO, 21st Street, Long Island, N.Y.

KUKLINSKI believes victim was carrying money but does not know how much or what the money was for. He was not told who George was meeting or why. George was known to sometime carry large sums of money but he did not carry a weapon to his knowledge. He doesn't know of any enemies or threats to George's life. Victim was traveling light and did not have any luggage, only a brown paper bag with possible change of shirt, etc.

KUKLINSKI stated that he was in debt to George for the sum of $7,500.00, however he cleared that debt by giving George two (2) checks in the amounts of $4,000.00 & $3,500.00 drawn on the FIRST NATIONAL BANK, Haworth, N.J. Both checks were from the SUNSET CO. account and made out to George Malliband in name. The checks were given to George Wednesday, Jan. 30th with agreement to hold them for a week before deposit.

In conclusion Mr. KUKLINSKI denied any knowledge regarding George's death. He said he first heard about from a fellow porno film salesman by the name of [   ] at CENTURY SALES, Pennsauken, N.J., Thursday evening, b6
February 7th.   b7c

Richard L. KUKLINSKI is a former Jersey City resident with past residences on Webster, Palisade & Danforth Avenues, also Congress and Sixteenth Streets.

Investigation to continue..........   b6
                                                                             b7c

52 TYPE NAME		53		54 DATE OF REPORT
Det.		PAGE 2 OF		1980
Signature		55 PCT/UNIT	56 SUPERVISOR	
		N/Homicide	Lt.	

RECORD ROOM COPY

1 SUSPECT(S)		2 PCT/UNIT No. Hom. Sq.	3 SECTION CASE NUMBER	4 FILE NUMBER 30696

MVR

7 Victim(s) NEW ADDRESS
GEORGE MOKLIBAND
1124 MIFFLIN St HUNTINGDON PA

5 CRIME OR SUBJECT MURDER	6 DATE OF CRIME 2/5/80	44 STATUS CRIME		
5A NEW CRIME IF CHANGED	6A NJ STATUTE 2C: 11-3	49A ADDITIONAL STOLEN PROPERTY VALUE		41A ADDITIONAL RECOVERED PROPERTY VALUE

ADDITIONAL VAL STOLEN PROPERTY	34A CURRENCY	36A JEWELRY	36A FURS	37A CLOTHING	38A AUTO	39A MISC.

LIST NAME ONLY OF PREVIOUS ACCUSED — COMPLETE INFORMATION ON NEW ACCUSED — INCLUDE ADDITIONAL PERPETRATORS — SUSPECTS — RECORD ALL DEVELOPMENTS SINCE LAST REPORT — EXPLAIN ANY CRIME CHANGE — LIST ADDITIONAL INTERVIEWS OF VICTIMS — PERSONS CONTACTED — WITNESSES — EVIDENCE — TECHNICAL SERVICES — STOLEN PROPERTY — RECOVERED PROPERTY — COURT ACTION

Accused: 46 NUMBER ACCUSED _____ 46A New accused _____ 47A ADULT _____ 48A JUVENILE _____ 49A RACE _____ 50A SEX _____ 51A DATE OF BIRTH

On 2/18/80 [   ] visited the
Homicide Office as previously reported, during this visit he was accompanied by [   ]
[   ] was interviewed and he related that the victim would
sometimes ask him to accompany him to N.Y.C. [   ] did most of the
driving as the victim did not like to drive. During one of these visits
to N.Y.C. the victim had an appointment with Mr. Kuklinski and did meet
Mr. Kuklinski in a small Chinese Restaurant across the street from Kuklinski's Office located at 125 Lafayette St. N.Y.C. [   ] stated that
Kuklinski shares this Office with A [   ]. After having a cup
of coffee in the Chinese Restaurant the three of them went to Kuklinski's
[   ] Office where Kuklinski and the victim discussed business and where
Kuklinski opened up a Brown Colored Brief Case that he was carrying.
[   ] did observe business papers in the Brief Case also a .38 Cal
Revolver, a 357 Magnum and did see Mr. Kuklinski with a small Caliber
Automatic which he carried in his pocket. It was also noted by [   ]
that during their visit to this Office, that [   ] was not there when
they first arrived but did come into the Office later, also that Kuklinski
has a key to this Office. [   ] owns a Printing Co at that location
where among other thing he prints and supplies boxes for Movie Film.
It is to noted that during interview with Richard Kuklinski on 2/11/80 he
stated that he had his other office , Sunset Co. 125 Lafayette St N.Y.C.
212 925 3770 and that he was a wholesaler of Clothing, also distributor.
Check shows " De Luxe Printing Card Co" located at this location and phone #
212 925 3000
Sgt.

52 TYPE NAME	8 BADGE	53 PAGE 1 OF 2 PAGES	54 DATE OF REPORT 2/28/80
Signature SG		55 PCT/UNIT Hom. SQ.	56 SUPERVISOR

RECORD ROOM COPY

1 SUSPECT(S)		2 PCT/UNIT NO. Hom Sq.	3 SECTION CASE NUMBER	4 FILE NUMBER 30696

Victim(s) NEW ADDRESS

George W. Malliband Jr.

5 CRIME OR SUBJECT Murder	6 DATE OF CRIME 2/5/80	1124 Mifflin St. Huntingdon PA.		
5A NEW CRIME IF CHANGED	6A NJ STATUTE 2C: 11-3	44 STATUS CRIME		45 STATUS CASE
		40A ADDITIONAL STOLEN PROPERTY VALUE		41A ADDITIONAL RECOVERED PROPERTY VALUE

ADDITIONAL VAL STOLEN PROPERTY	34A CURRENCY	35A JEWELRY	36A FURS	37A CLOTHING	38A AUTO	39A MISC.

LIST NAME ONLY OF PREVIOUS ACCUSED — COMPLETE INFORMATION ON NEW ACCUSED — INCLUDE ADDITIONAL PERPETRATORS — SUSPECTS — RECORD ALL DEVELOPMENTS SINCE LAST REPORT — EXPLAIN ANY CRIME CHANGE — LIST ADDITIONAL INTERVIEWS OF VICTIMS — PERSONS CONTACTED — WITNESSES — EVIDENCE — TECHNICAL SERVICES — STOLEN PROPERTY — RECOVERED PROPERTY — COURT ACTION

Accused: 46 NUMBER ACCUSED _____ 46A New accused _____ 47A ADULT _____ 48A JUVENILE _____ 49A RACE _____ 50A SEX _____ 51A DATE OF BIRTH

[_____] also related that the victim visited N.Y.C. about every two weeks and picked up about 25 Cases of Movie Film from a Processor in Queens N.Y., name and address unknown. Victim paid approximately $425.00 to $450.00 per Case, with 100 reels of Film in each case; he would then resell them for about $500.00 to $575.00 Per Case.

[_____] gave the following dimensions (estimated) of these cases: 18" High 18" Long, and 2' Deep, and each case weighing about 25 pounds. He also stated when the victim visited N.Y.C. , the he would stay at the Skyline Motor Inn. A Check with the phone directory shows this Motel to be located at 10 Ave. & 50th St. N.Y.C. Phone 212 586 3400.

At 1400 Hours 2/20/80 the U/S had a telephone conversation with [_____] who stated that on 1/31/80 between 7:00 P.M. and 8:00 PM. the victim stopped at his home and asked to see [_____]. [_____] told the victim that [_____] was not at home. The victim told him that he was going to N.Y.C. and coming right back the next day. On 2/1/80 [_____] received a phone call from the victim who stated that he was alone in the office and that he was waiting for someone to come into the office. When [_____] asked him where Richard Kuklinski was , the victim stated that he had walked up the street a short time ago. [_____] phone call with the victim was between 10:00 AM and x noon on 2/1/80. Office in question not known at this time, as Kuklinski has an Office at 428 B Old Hook Road Emerson N.J., 125 Lafayette St. N.Y.C and also has a business Phone at his home, 169 Sunset St. Dumont, Phone 385 5548.

Sgt. [_____]

52 TYPE NAME	58 BADGE	53 PAGE 2 OF 2 PAGES	54 DATE OF REPORT 2/20/80
Signature		55 PCT/UNIT Hom. Sq.	56 SUPERVISOR AP

Image Gallery

Richard and Barbara

Richard and his children

Richard and Barbara with their two daughters

Richard as a young boy

Robert Prongay

Aka Mr Softee

Gary Smith   Danny Deppner

Below: George Malliband

Barbara and Richard

HBO Specials

The Iceman Tapes: Conversations with a killer (1992).
HBO, aired 1992 - https://www.imdb.com/title/tt0874289/

The Iceman Confesses: Secrets of a Mafia Hitman (2001).
HBO, aired 2001 - https://www.imdb.com/title/tt0347228/

The Iceman – feature length film

Amazon Prime have released a film dramatizing the life of Richard 'The Iceman' Kuklinski, it is mostly accurate but not completely. Some events have been altered for dramatic effect.

Description

"Chronicles the life of real-life contract killer Richard Kuklinski, who was eventually caught and convicted in 1986. Perhaps most shocking of all was his family's total ignorance as to his real career."
Directed by Ariel Vromen
Starring Winona Ryder as Barbara Kuklinski & Michael Shannon as Richard Kuklinski

It can be watched here -
https://www.amazon.co.uk/gp/video/detail/B085L192CJ/ref=atv_dp_share_cu_r

Further Reading

The Iceman: The True Story of a Cold-Blooded Killer by Anthony Bruno.

A well informed, professionally written book.

The topics and events covered in this book stick to the facts of the Kuklinski case. Most claims in this book can verified by other supporting documentation.

Definitely a good read for those who would like to investigate the case from other angles. Perfect for anyone wanting to get an idea of how Richard operated on a day-to-day basis, along with an insight into the undercover investigation that resulted in his capture.

Immortal Monster by Anthony Bruno

A short follow up book that discusses Richards later claims to murder and the plausibility of those claims. A quick and easy read.

The Iceman: Confessions of a contract killer by Philip Carlo

A relatively detailed book to be taken with a pinch of salt!

Although this book is filled with information and many bold claims, the validity of such claims is very questionable. There are murders described in depth that cannot be linked to any type of proof or evidence to actual events. There are no records of such cases in criminal databases either. The more famous claims to contracted hits such as those of Castellano and Hoffa for example seem to have no basis in reality and Richards version of events contradict the known facts of the crime scene or case information held by Law Enforcement.

To gain a look into Richards home life with his family this book does offer greater insight than others.

Kuklinski Family Obituaries

&

Other records of death

Find a Grave, database and images
(https://www.findagrave.com : accessed 18 January 2021),
memorial page for Anna McNally (31 Jan 1911–21 Mar
1972), Find a Grave Memorial no. 99066634, citing Holy
Cross Cemetery, North Arlington, Bergen County, New
Jersey, USA ; Maintained by Big Ern
(contributor 46620889) .

Find a Grave, database and images
(https://www.findagrave.com : accessed 18 January 2021),
memorial page for Florian Kuklinski (11 Apr 1933–1 Feb
1941), Find a Grave Memorial no. 98307987, citing Holy
Cross Cemetery, North Arlington, Bergen County, New
Jersey, USA ; Maintained by Big Ern
(contributor 46620889) .

Find a Grave, database and images
(https://www.findagrave.com : accessed 18 January 2021),
memorial page for Jan "John" Kuklinski (21 Sep 1884–14
Apr 1941), Find a Grave Memorial no. 22865923, citing
Holy Name Cemetery, Jersey City, Hudson County, New
Jersey, USA ; Maintained by Jean Dupon
(contributor 46556107) .

Find a Grave, database and images
(https://www.findagrave.com : accessed 18 January 2021),
memorial page for John F. Kuklinski (3 Dec 1914–15 Feb
2005), Find a Grave Memorial no. 98307382, citing Holy

Cross Cemetery, North Arlington, Bergen County, New Jersey, USA ; Maintained by Big Ern (contributor 46620889) .

Find a Grave, database and images (https://www.findagrave.com : accessed 18 January 2021), memorial page for Joseph Michael Kuklinski (5 May 1944–22 Sep 2003), Find a Grave Memorial no. 46846417, ; Maintained by Princess Kim (contributor 46869845) Unknown.

Find a Grave, database and images (https://www.findagrave.com : accessed 18 January 2021), memorial page for Louis Masgay (11 Apr 1931–1 Jul 1981), Find a Grave Memorial no. 122617028, ; Maintained by W H (contributor 46776106) Unknown.

Find a Grave, database and images (https://www.findagrave.com : accessed 18 January 2021), memorial page for Maryanna "Mary" Kuklinski (1888–18 Jul 1950), Find a Grave Memorial no. 22865924, citing Holy Name Cemetery, Jersey City, Hudson County, New Jersey, USA ; Maintained by Jean Dupon (contributor 46556107) .

Find a Grave, database and images (https://www.findagrave.com : accessed 18 January 2021), memorial page for Peter A Calabro (1943–1980), Find a Grave Memorial no. 219531556, citing Madonna Cemetery, Fort Lee, Bergen County, New Jersey, USA ; Maintained by Mark Pollack (contributor 50249363) .

Find a Grave, database and images (https://www.findagrave.com : accessed 18 January 2021), memorial page for Richard Leonard "Iceman" Kuklinski (11 Apr 1935–5 Mar 2006), Find a Grave Memorial no. 13709759, ; Maintained by Find A Grave Cremated, Ashes given to family or friend.

Find a Grave, database and images (https://www.findagrave.com : accessed 18 January 2021), memorial page for Roberta Florence Kuklinski Boyle (27 Sep 1942–11 Dec 2010), Find a Grave Memorial no. 174278721, citing Holy Cross Cemetery, North Arlington, Bergen County, New Jersey, USA ; Maintained by Ed Thurman (contributor 46846073) .

Find a Grave, database and images (https://www.findagrave.com : accessed 18 January 2021), memorial page for Robert J. Prongay (unknown–Aug 1984), Find a Grave Memorial no. 99448703, citing Holy Cross Cemetery, North Arlington, Bergen County, New Jersey, USA ; Maintained by Find a Grave (contributor 8) .

Find a Grave, database and images (https://www.findagrave.com : accessed 18 January 2021), memorial page for Stanley Kuklinski (22 Dec 1906–Jan 1977), Find a Grave Memorial no. 98307995, citing Holy Cross Cemetery, North Arlington, Bergen County, New Jersey, USA ; Maintained by Big Ern (contributor 46620889) .

Find a Grave, database and images (https://www.findagrave.com : accessed 18 January 2021), memorial page for Stella Kuklinski Gallas (1907–Feb 1963), Find a Grave Memorial no. 209157812, citing Holy Cross Cemetery, North Arlington, Bergen County, New Jersey, USA ; Maintained by Tami Glock (contributor 46872676) .

US social security death index. Robert Prongay 1945 - 1984. Social Security Administration (SSA) retrieved from

- https://www.myheritage.com/research/record-10002-
15832332-/robert-prongay-in-us-social-security-death-
index-ssdi?indId=externalindividual-
7e4d8484f64ccab867e4536111c3ffad&trn=partner_Geni&t
rp=logged_out_matches_module Accessed: 28 Dec 2020

Reference

Baskin-Sommers AR, Curtin JJ, Newman JP. Specifying
the Attentional Selection That Moderates the Fearlessness
of Psychopathic Offenders. Psychological Science.
2011;22(2):226-234. doi:10.1177/0956797610396227

Bruno, A. (2013) [1993]. The Iceman: The True Story of a
Cold-Blooded Killer. ROBERT HALE LTD.
ISBN9780709052722.

Bruno, A. (2018) [2011]. Immortal Monster. Dark Horse
Multimedia Inc., Virginia. ISBN Kindle edition:
9781949226034

Camisa, H. Franklin, J. (2003). Inside Out: Fifty Years
Behind the Walls of New Jersey's Trenton State Prison.
Windsor Press and Publishing. P. 247. ISBN097647309,
9780972647304.

Crystal Ponti. (2020). The Iceman': An Undercover Agent
Reflects on Taking Down Notorious Hitman Richard
Kuklinski. A+E Networks. Retrieved from -
https://www.aetv.com/real-crime/the-iceman-richard-
kuklinski-hitman. Accessed: 04 Jan 2021

Dolan, J.(Dec 18 1986) Man Charged With Killing
Associates, Accomplices In Illegal Business Deals. AP
News. Retrieved from -
https://apnews.com/article/fd57cb7179ef65c91761c3ceeeab
53dd Accessed: 04 Jan 2021

Galante, P. (2018) National security archive, Federal
Bureau of Investigation. Retrieved from -
https://archive.org/details/RichardKuklinski/Richard%20K
uklinski%2001. Accessed: 28 Dec 2020.

Hentoff, N. (1997) POLICING THE POLICE. Washington Post Archives. November 15, 1997

Iceman: Suspected in 5 deaths arrested (Dec 18, 1986). The Montreal Gazette. Retrieved from - https://news.google.com/newspapers?id=i1kiAAAAIBAJ& pg=952,4213260&hl=en. Accessed: 04 Jan 2021
  ISSN 0006-3223.
https://doi.org/10.1016/j.biopsych.2009.07.035.

Jacobs, A. (2003) Reality Tv Confession Leads to Real Life Conviction. New York Times. Section B, P1. Retrieved from - https://www.nytimes.com/2003/02/21/nyregion/reality-tv-confession-leads-to-real-life-conviction.html Accessed: 04 Jan 2021

Jayne Leonard, (2020). What to know about abandonment issues. Medical News Today. Retrieved from - https://www.medicalnewstoday.com/articles/abandonment-issues Accessed on 28 Dec 2020

Jerry Capeci, May 5, 2005. Case Builds Against Accused 'Mafia Cops' Retrieved from - https://web.archive.org/web/20201209060334/https://www.nysun.com/new-york/case-builds-against-accused-mafia-cops/13349/. Accessed 28 Dec 2020

Jersey City Police Department. (1980) Supplementary Investigation Report. Kuklinski, #30696-80. Homicide of G, Malliband. Federal Bureau of Investigation. National Security Archive. (2018)

Jersey man charged in 5 murders linked with fake business deals. New York Times. Dec 8, 1986, Section B, Page8 retrieved from -

https://www.nytimes.com/1986/12/18/nyregion/jersey-man-charged-in-5-murders-linked-with-fake-business-deals.html

Joseph P. Newman, John J. Curtin, Jeremy D. Bertsch, Arielle R. Baskin-Sommers. Attention Moderates the Fearlessness of Psychopathic Offenders. Biological Psychiatry. 2010; 67, (1):66-70.

Kimura Y, Yoshino A, Takahashi Y, Nomura S. Interhemispheric difference in emotional response without awareness. Physiol Behav. 2004 Sep 30;82(4):727-31. doi: 10.1016/j.physbeh.2004.06.010. PMID: 15327923.

Martin, Douglas. "Richard Kuklinski, 70, a Killer Of Many People and Many Ways." *New York Times*, 9 Mar. 2006, p. C18(L). *Gale OneFile: News*, link.gale.com/apps/doc/A142989908/STND?u=tou&sid=STND&xid=087873a8. Accessed: 5 Jan. 2021.

N.D. (1970). Jersey City Man Arrested In Death of 12-Year-Old Girl. The New York Times. Archived. Retrieved from - https://www.nytimes.com/1970/09/16/archives/jersey-city-man-arrested-in-death-of-12yearold-girl.html. Accessed on 04 Dec 2020

New York Times (1972). Eboli Is 15th Gangland Victim in a Year. New York Times Archives. (July 17, 1972) P:20

NJ Herald (1986). Murder Charges Levelled 2 county men among victims. New Jersey Herald Archives.18 December 1986.

Pace, E. (1971). Bar Owner Found Shot to Death In Car in Midtown Parking Lot. New York Times Archives. December 25, 1971.

Robert D. McFadden, (1984) 5 EX-CITY POLICEMEN INVESTIGATED IN REPORTED SALE OF DATA TO MOB. New York Times Archives. April 9, 1984, Section B, P.3.

Smothers, R. (1986) WITNESS DESCRIBES AID TO GAMBINO CAR-THEFT RING BY OFFICERS. New York Times Archives. Jan. 14, 1986. Section B, P:2

Stantini v. U.S., 97 CV 3659 (ILG), 97 CV 6683 (ILG) (E.D.N.Y. Mar. 3, 2003)

State Vs. Kuklinski (1988) Superior Court of New Jersey, Law Division, Bergen County. Robert J. Carroll, Deputy Attorney General. Neal M. Frank Senior Trial Attorney. (17 March 1988)

The New York Times (1992). A New John Guido for the Police. New York Times Archives. June 20, 1992. Section 1, P:22

Toth, R. Ostrow, R. (1988). Russian Mafia: KGB Steers Criminals to U.S. Careers. Los Angeles Times Archives. (Feb 16, 1988)

United States. (1976). *Organized crime: report of the task force on organized crime*. Dept. of Justice Law Enforcement Assistance Administration National Advisory Committee on Criminal Justice Standards and Goals: For sale by the Supt. of Docs. U.S. Govt. Print. Off.